DATE DUE

The Money Instruction Book

Because Money Doesn't Come with Instructions

© 2016 Max Horne

WRITE BUSINESS RESULTS

This book was produced in collaboration with Write Business Results Ltd.
www.writebusinessresults.com / info@writebusinessresults.com

Contents

Introduction

You are the millennials, the first young adults of the new century. Unlike your parents and grandparents, you live in the real world and the virtual world. Constant connection, not just with your friends, but nationally and internationally, is probably one of your greatest priorities, and you want the instant gratification of Snapchat, Instagram, Twitter, and Facebook.

You might live in the fantastic, magical, cybernetic world of the Cloud, but you need to get your head out of the clouds when it comes to managing the one thing you most probably have seen little of in your sixteen, seventeen or eighteen years: money!

Money is talked about all the time, but little of any real value is actually said. It is still a hush-hush subject. You might know how much Ronaldo earns in a year, or how many likes Kim

Kardashian's latest Instagram post got, but ask your parents or teachers what they earn or how much they have in the bank, and you will be told in no uncertain terms to mind your own business. As a result, most young people give little thought to their parent's jobs or careers, know how mum and dad manage their money, or how they balance their accounts each month.

How many of you have your own bank account, or savings account, and know how to read your statement, or know what compound interest is? The language surrounding money consists of acronyms from APR (Annual Percentage Rate) to STO (Standing Order), and reams of mind-boggling financial gobbledygook. Unless you are studying accountancy at A level, the majority of you probably have little idea of how to look after your money, when it eventually comes your way. It is not a big part of the curriculum, only being taught as part of citizenship classes in the past few years. You may have been taught tricky equations and logarithms but have never been shown how to fill in a tax return.

Every child in the United Kingdom is entitled to a free education up to the age of eighteen. This is your birthright, but not every child is born equal. Some of you reading this book may have had a privileged upbringing and enjoyed plenty of spoils, including a comfortable home, fashionable clothes and foreign holidays. Some of you will be entirely aware of the cost of living, have to share with brothers and sisters, and be content with less. And some of you know what it means to be poor, when it is a struggle for your parents to put food on the table.

Whatever your experience, the concept of money will have been introduced to you at an early age, when you stood at the checkout in the supermarket begging for the sweets strategically placed at your eye level, but you will not necessarily have grown up with an understanding of where the money comes from. You may be given pocket money or an allowance, and either save it or spend it, knowing you will get more next week. You may have to earn your pocket money and then the chances are you will appreciate and respect the rewards of your hard work.

Now it is time to leave school, you will be planning on getting a job and a weekly wage, or leaving home for university, or college, and a career, when you graduate. You may be excited at the prospect, or petrified by the idea of standing on your own two feet, paying your own rent and tuition fees. Whatever you choose to do, you will soon experience the ebb and flow of money and need to know how to manage it, both in the short-term and in the long run.

"The long run," I hear you say, in horror. "Why would I want to think about next year, let alone my retirement? I'm just looking forward to finally getting to Glastonbury or to seeing the Champions League Final. I want to hang out at festivals, bars, see the world. What do I want with a book about mortgages and pensions?"

STOP! Hold it right there. Don't shut this book before we have begun! Money is a serious business, but I am not going to bore you with budgets. After all, I detest the word 'budget', as you will soon discover. I know you want your independence, freedom, the opportunity of new events, and a smartphone, and this is why I have devised the 'bucket list'. My bucket list is not a long list of all the amazing experiences you may want before you die, although it could well be. It is more a way to think about your money and how to make it work for you; now, next year and always. Just as you need to learn to drive, take your theory and practical test before you are allowed to take a car on the road, think of this book in the same way; a license to handle money!

This book is not a get rich quick book but the result of the many observations I have made during a lifelong career of giving financial advice. Some people make the right decisions and become spectacularly wealthy. Others make the wrong decisions and, consequently, become poor. We all have a desire for success and a fear of failure and sometimes we do make mistakes and believe me, I have made a few along the way myself.

So who am I to be giving you this advice? I left home in the Borders of Scotland to attend college in Newcastle. I had saved up enough money from a regular paper round and from doing odd jobs, such as seasonal farm work and labouring on a building site during the school summer holidays, to buy a small car that was my pride and joy. The golden rule my parents enforced was that I had to maintain the car and pay for all the costs of running it myself. After all, they were giving me an allowance to cover the costs of my rent, food and other expenses at college, and they expected me to use some of my savings to pay for any 'luxuries' I wanted.

My financial planning was a disaster! Instead of giving me the money on a monthly basis, my parents gave me the money each term in a lump sum. I promptly spent that money on buying new shiny parts for my car and a healthy dose of partying. The result was what I call 'too much month left for the money' and I quickly became 'broke.' I needed to change my ways.

The next term the same pattern emerged, but with one difference. I left my car at home and decided to take public transport everywhere, eliminating my motoring costs for the rest of that year. Nevertheless, I approached graduation with just £1 in my pocket to last me for the final three weeks.

Some of you are acquainted with failure and know the 'fringe benefits.' A string of poor marks may well have made you work harder for your next exam. And some of you may have been brought up with a very sensible approach to everything you do from consistently winning prizes for the sports team to achieving great grades playing the piano and always saving your pocket money. Some of you are disciplined by nature, and some have to learn to be disciplined. In the big wide world there is no one to tell you not to run in the corridor, or how to spend wisely.

Our attitudes to money are imprinted on our DNA. We can't change this, but we can know ourselves and watch out for the pitfalls. One of the biggest challenges you are about to face is temptation. When you are presented with your first week, or month's, pay packet or join fresher's week at university, you will suddenly have more spending power than you have ever had before. You will be offered a student loan, credit cards and overdrafts. If you don't learn how to manage your money now, you could end up not just owing thousands of pounds but suffering a thousand different petty humiliations and hardships.

Unlike your parents, you are the first generation that needs to contend with the heavy price of student debt and an aging population. You might be carefree, or you might be frightened, impulsive or careless. You might want a simple life, or to be a millionaire. Every expectation has a price and if you follow my life plan of achievable goals through school and in the workplace, you could achieve great things. But, whatever your lot in life, you will certainly be happier for never fearing poverty.

 **KEY TAKEAWAYS**

- Money is a serious topic that's seldom talked about in a serious way (except when you run out of it). Let's talk (and think) about it.

- This book isn't a get rich quick plan, instead it's all about it's all about giving you sound financial info that'll help you out in the future (whether you want to get rich or not). giving you sound financial info that'll help you out in the future (whether you want to get rich or not.)

1 WHAT DOES MONEY MEAN TO YOU?

What is money?

Like the Cloud and time, money is a manmade concept, a manmade idea and not something natural or organic. Money clearly does not grow on trees! Throughout history, money has been attached to something material, something you can touch, like gold. The pound notes in your pocket are linked to bars of gold bullion kept in vaults by the banks, but few of us ever see such wealth and certainly never get to touch a nugget of gold, let alone a bar.

In fact, there is a glittering stash of gold bars worth a whopping £156 billion, stored in an old canteen deep below the streets of the London by the Bank of England. In New York, the Federal Reserve keep their gold in an underground vault with no doors.

Entry is through a narrow passageway cut in a steel cylinder that vertically revolves and the gold in handled by robots.

In the modern world, where we access our banks online and never have to pass through the high street door, paper money is used less and less. Pound coins, five, 10 and 20 pound notes have almost been replaced by plastic, linked directly to your account at the bank, dispensing with the need for cash. One swipe of a debit card buys a cup of coffee without the need to count your change.

Do we really understand money? Apparently not. If we did, people would be more open about it and talk to their children more openly. In our society, the subject is off limits; it is taboo. People are embarrassed and secretive about money, and it is the cause of many arguments and stress between both parents and their children.

What does money mean to you?

From physical pound notes in your pocket to numbers in the bank, what does money mean to you? As a teenager still in school it probably means independence, the ability to have a little freedom to go out and spend time with your friends.

But let's look at the bigger picture. Money means different things to different people, depending on who we become as we search for our place in the world.

For some it means status or fame; they want to be seen to have lots of money as proof of their success. They want to see six-figure balances at the bottom of their bank statement and the balance regularly increasing. For others, actual wealth is not important. It means everything money can buy over their lifetime, from a home full of technological gadgets, or a smart car, to traveling the world, or saving the planet.

There is no escaping from it; everyone, from the most selfless amongst us to the most materialistic, needs money. We are all consumers, one way or another. One of the questions this will help you answer, is what does money mean to you, personally? It's important you give this some thought over the coming days, weeks, months, even years; basically until you're able to pinpoint how money could be important to you as you grow and move through life.

What do you want money for?

Today you may want money in the short term to go shopping

and to spend the weekends with your friends. You may have set your sights on a new outfit or be saving up for a smartphone or an iPad. You could well have a weekend or holiday job and be looking forward to driving lessons or putting money away to travel.

In the long term, you may have already thought about all the different things you will do at university or college. Once you have graduated, you could eventually want a home you can call your own, and a new car. You may want money to travel the big, wide world and see and experience different cultures. Or you might see money as the essential ingredient to making a family and to settling down. Some of you might want money to help people less fortunate, and some of you might see it as the means to escape the city or live by the sea.

Whatever you want money for, it's important that you are

aware. If you don't know what you might want money for, you can't possible plan to get what you want. And that - going through life never getting what you really want - is one of the biggest travesties. In preparing and planning for your money, you are simply allowing yourself the things or experiences that could make you happy. Money isn't the be all and end all - there is so much more to life than worrying about money - but it is the tool that will get you to where you want to go.

How much money do you need?

What we want and what we need are two different things. What you actually need to survive is a roof over your head, clothes on your back and food on the table from the day you leave home and pay your own way, to the day your hair is grey, and your skin is wrinkled, and you die. The bigger the roof, the fancier the clothes and the more exclusive the food, the more money you will want.

Is it possible to live without spending any cash whatsoever? After becoming disillusioned with consumer society, one man decided to give it a try. He lived in a caravan he picked up for free and grew his own food. He still had to spend £360 on solar panels to generate heat and light, proving it is never entirely workable. However, he showed us just how little we really need.

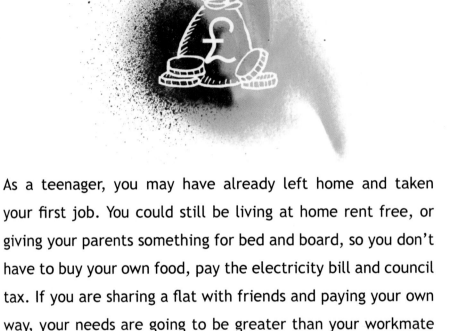

As a teenager, you may have already left home and taken your first job. You could still be living at home rent free, or giving your parents something for bed and board, so you don't have to buy your own food, pay the electricity bill and council tax. If you are sharing a flat with friends and paying your own way, your needs are going to be greater than your workmate who is still living at home. You will need to pay your national insurance, tax and pension contributions. Whatever's left is yours to save or spend.

If you are planning on further education, university or college, your needs will be the same as others on your course. You will have to pay rent whether you are in halls of residence or sharing a private house or flat. You will have to pay your tuition fees and buy your books and your laptop; once a luxury but now a necessity for any degree course. On top of that, you will need money for food, to get around, and essential clothes. These are your basic needs.

Nights out in bars, drinking pints and cocktails, weekend long parties, takeaway pizzas and curries, gigs and festivals are all part of the experience, but they are luxuries. These are the things you want, not the things you need.

How has money shaped you?

What is your attitude to money? However little or however much has come your way in your short lifetime, it will have already shaped your opinion. Over the years, in my dealings with people and their money, I have become more and more convinced your attitude to money is formed not only by your parents but by your environment and circumstances, by the time you are just seven-years-old.

Your childhood experiences will make you cautious or careless. A client of mine told me her father died when she was very young. Her mother struggled on low earnings to keep a roof over their heads, and there was little food to eat. The family often had nothing but porridge for days on end. As a result, this woman, who grew up to be a university professor, became one of the most amazing savers you could meet.

She put the maximum she could into her pension pot and saved at least a third of her income. She lived life to the full, but always sought out a bargain, never paying a penny more than she had to. When she retired, she found it difficult to stop saving and start spending. She gradually made the adjustment, excitedly traveling to far-flung places, enjoying the spoils of her good sense.

Likewise, my wife, brought up in post-war Germany, remembers the lessons learned from her wise grandmother. With little money to spare, they would walk from the village where she lived to the nearest market town. They walked for about three miles; quite a challenge for a small child. Having saved a bus fare, they would buy fresh vegetables and food to last the week and then ride home with the heavy shopping bags. As a result, my wife has always been cautious, saving money wherever she can.

At the other end of the spectrum I come across some people who have all the trappings of wealth but who have neither the income or savings to support their expenses. They live in a posh part of town with shiny, new cars parked in the driveway, wear designer clothes, often take long haul holidays but are living way beyond their means.

If you were to lift the veil of secrecy you will find their homes are mortgaged to the hilt, they don't have the money in the bank to pay for their lavish lifestyle, and they are often maxed out on their credit cards. These people grew up at a time when money was easy, and the banks encouraged everyone to borrow.

Have you read the story of the Emperor's New Clothes; the metaphor for anything that smacks of pretentiousness? People living way beyond their income belong to all economic groups of society. They can be executives, professionals or unskilled workers. However, this attitude differs from country to country. The British and American's have developed a spending culture, caught up in the frenzy of 'must have' and 'must have it now', unlike their German counterparts who are more inclined to save around a fifth of their income for the future.

Many of our beliefs around money are passed down from our parents and, in turn, from their parents. Whether you are careful with money or extravagant will essentially come from your inner beliefs and from observing your parents as you grow up. Some of the happiest homes are where parents have no real money worries, are comfortable with their earnings, and with everything they have, from the house you live in to where you go on holiday. If that describes your parents, you are starting out on a better footing than many of your friends who may live in a bigger house and have so much more than you. Behind the scenes, their parent's wealth might be real, or it could be an illusion. They could be struggling to afford their pipedreams and are heavily in debt.

You will also be influenced by your family values, the moral principles that guide your life. Your parents will have instilled in you at a very early age acceptable standards of behaviour, a general code of conduct. This also extends to your morals. And your morals, to a certain extent, guide what your relationship with money will be over your lifetime.

Pastimes such as gambling and betting may be morally unacceptable in your family. This will be passed down, and you will see the stupidity in such a waste of money. However, the family that condones gambling and betting sees this as a chance to get rich quick to solve all of their money problems. Every week we see new millionaires created by the lottery and dream of it being us.

We are all different and attach a different meaning to money. For many that association can be negative: fear, greed and anxiety. These beliefs about money are most likely formed in childhood and passed on through the experiences of our immediate family and school friends. So what does money mean to you? Does it mean safety and security; a roof over your head and food on the table? Does it mean the freedom to choose how you want to live your life, where you live, and what type of work you do? Does it mean power, in the sense that no one can control and hurt you? Or does it mean helping the family and seeing them succeed? Is it simply the route to the things you want?

For most people, it is a healthy combination of all of the above.

Attitudes to money can be inherited. You may be part of a family of spenders, or a family of savers, and therefore have money habits just like mum and dad. Or the opposite, depending upon your money-related experiences.

Take the example of two sisters. They were brought up identically, with the same family values. They had the same education and the same amount of pocket money each week. One was encouraged to save from an early age and praised for her efforts, but the younger sister was left to her own devices. The first grew up to be a saver, cautiously guarding her income, just like her mother, and the other a spender who blatantly had little regard for her money, just like her father.

You will better understand your own values, whether you are proud of yourself, ashamed of yourself or couldn't care less, as soon as you start earning your own money. Blaming mum and dad stops the day you are old enough to drive and start to take control.

The great British taboo

Money is something we are all fascinated and governed by, and yet it is very British not actually to talk about it. This concept goes back several centuries in that we did not tell people how much money we had in our wallets, purses and pockets for fear of being attacked and robbed by pickpockets or highwaymen. There is still, to this day, a great fear of losing money, and a dramatic sense of loss and guilt surrounding anything from a fifty pence piece dropped in the playground, to huge losses on the stock exchange.

As children, we often save our money in 'piggy banks' or money boxes, and we often conceal these in ingenious hiding places, in case other people, including our brothers and sisters, want to 'borrow' our money. We are always reluctant to lend, for fear of not being paid back. This all starts at an early age, but the habit continues as we grow into adulthood.

You've probably never asked your parents how much money they have in their bank accounts because you almost instinctively know the answer would be, "mind your own business." Our parents might help us out with a gift of money for different things throughout our

lifetime, whether it is to purchase a laptop for school, your first car, extra money for college, or help with the deposit for a house. Inevitably the gift is accompanied by the phrase, "Here is a little something for you," and they never say, "Here is my last penny."

The secrecy continues as your parents move up the career

ladder or change jobs, usually for a higher salary, but they won't tell you what those salaries are. Even successful parents put up a wall of silence. This mystery around earnings repeats itself as we, in turn, conceal what we earn from colleagues in the workplace or our friends. We will occasionally find a close friend being more open, sharing confidences. Some people are boastful, presuming they are earning more than you, and a few are good friends who share all their concerns.

At a school reunion, a class of friends got together ten years after they had all left school. They were now aged 27 and were all in work. One of their schoolmates arrived driving a Ferrari with a stunning, supermodel of a girlfriend. "Who is that?" asked the rest of the class. Nobody could remember him being at school. As it transpired, it was Johnny, the nerd in the corner who no one paid any attention to. He never played sports, he never talked to the girls or had any friends. He came from an average family, had the worst haircut and always looked a mess in hand-me-down clothes. Day and night he stared at a computer screen and despite his good grades, he remained invisible; he slipped under the radar.

It turned out Johnny had done well at school and gone on to a top university, graduated with a first-class honours degree in mathematics and then gone to work as a trader in the City of London with one of the world's largest banks. He had quickly risen to the top of his profession and was paid a huge salary and bonus. Wearing the latest Italian designer suit, and a smart haircut, he was the picture of success.

The reaction amongst his peers was mixed. Some thought it was amazing that one of their own had done so well. Others were jealous of his effective 'rags-to-riches' story. Johnny had never disclosed his secret ambition to anyone. It was not surprising no one recognised him.

Working with colleagues inevitably brings up the subject of money, but it is more about the cost of living than how much we earn. There is still huge secrecy among workers as to how much individual earns, unless you are a doctor, a train driver, a teacher, in the army or navy, or a civil servant, where you salary is public knowledge. If you start work in the private sector, it is common for people in the same office to get paid at different rates, due to different skill levels, value to the employer and what rate of pay you negotiated from the outset.

The money someone borrows to buy a house or car and what they owe on a credit card is nearly always a matter of privacy. The majority of individuals who have credit-card debt, do not admit it, and rarely own up when they struggle to make repayments. They do not confess to the fact they have borrowed far too much for fear they will be marked out as being reckless and their debt exposed.

They never tell the truth about money to family or friends. Other cultures are far more open. In the banks in Greece, you are hardly ever given privacy when talking to the manager about your money. Everyone gathers round to hear the discussion and see how much you have in your account. On the one hand it may seem rude, but on the other, if a friend or neighbour is in trouble, someone inevitably steps in to help.

The other area of secrecy is when an individual saves up money in an account and doesn't tell anyone else about it. Many married women, or women in a partnership, will have set up a separate bank account to which they add money on a regular basis as an escape fund or a fund over which they have total control. Historically, women were not allowed bank accounts and their husbands or male relatives took control over any money they may have inherited. Men were the main breadwinners and allocated housekeeping to their wives, and a small allowance called 'pin money' for their clothes.

Although society has changed and women go to work, some men still see it as their role to make all the decisions regarding the family's spending or investments. It is not uncommon for men to use money to bully and control a wife or girlfriend's spending by not giving them access to money. Women feel more secure when they have some money of their own, especially if the marriage or relationship goes wrong and they need to get away. Regardless of whether or not a couple have a joint bank account for combined expenses, everyone should keep their autonomy with their own savings account; men and women alike.

Making your money work for you

We have established what you need money for and what you want money for, but how do you manage your money when you have actually got some. The problems and the solutions are the same whether you are on a low wage stacking shelves in a supermarket, training as a hairdresser, learning to drive a train, becoming a doctor, a teacher, a graphic designer, a gardener, a lawyer or financial adviser. You will have a certain amount of money coming in and you will have to make it cover the cost of living: your needs, and life's luxuries, your wants and crucially, your savings.

We are now living in an age with the highest number of people declaring themselves bankrupt as a result of massive debt, and the culture of saving has all but disappeared. You could say,

"I will never let that happen to me," but any minute now you are going to be under enormous pressure to start borrowing as you are introduced to loans, credit cards and overdrafts. Before you even know what your first monthly salary will be, you could be swimming in debt. Those friendly faces offering you money during fresher's week will turn into sharks the day you graduate.

We are surrounded by consumer advertising, telling us what we must buy, from handbags to vacuum cleaners, if we are to be seen as one of the beautiful people. Lifestyle advertising tempts us to sun-kissed islands and rooftop bars, not to a caravan in a lacklustre resort. We are constantly reminded, online and offline, to spend, never save, and never mind the consequences.

One young couple who met at university, graduated, found jobs in the same town, fell in love and decided to get married. They diligently saved until they had enough for a deposit on a house and their wedding. No small achievement. They applied to the bank for a mortgage and were refused. Ouch! They weren't expecting this. They had money in the bank and good jobs, but a credit search revealed that when at university they had defaulted on their credit card payments for three consecutive months.

Juggling their finances, they had put off paying the bill until the next student loan cheque came in. The effect of their carelessness, enjoying the heady, carefree days of their youth, will be hard to shake off, as they now have a history of poor credit.

This all sounds like doom and gloom, but the warning bells I am sounding now are intended to spare you from many serious problems you could encounter as you journey through life. Has anyone ever told you what it means to be bankrupt? When debts have mounted up to a point where repayments cannot be met, and the credit companies are knocking at the door, a person can be declared bankrupt.

Bankruptcy is a legal status that usually lasts for a year but the effects can last a lifetime. Your non-essential property and possessions, your things, and any money over and above what you need to live on, are used to pay off your creditors, those people you owe money to. At the end of the bankruptcy period, most debts are canceled.

In the short term you might lose your television, your laptop, your watch, and jewellery; anything which can be sold, but you are not allowed to use your bank account, building society account or credit cards and will find it very hard to get credit in the future.

You are not even able to hire a car. Being bankrupt is not an ennobling experience. There is a great stigma attached to bankruptcy, and the reality is very painful. As the writer, Charles Dickens of Oliver Twist fame, said, "Annual income £20, annual expenditure £19.06, result – happiness. Annual income £20, annual expenditure £20.06, result – misery."

In my job as an Independent Financial Adviser I am used to talking to clients about the concept of putting money into buckets, of dividing their income, rather than about budgeting.

Simply visualise four, shiny, new buckets.

The first bucket is the spending bucket and is used to accumulate money for everyday items, such as food, council taxes, light and heat, water, and rent. As your responsibilities grow, this will also cover mortgage payments, life insurance, property and buildings insurance, replacement clothing, travel expenses, petrol, and car insurance. Money flows in and flow out of this bucket on a regular basis.

The second bucket is the savings bucket. This is where you place monies that are going to be used for your short to medium-term needs. This is where you put your emergency fund and the money you are saving for a car or holiday and, in time, a deposit for a house. This is the bucket where most discipline is needed, as money in this bucket is easily accessible and is at the greatest risk of temptation to use for an impulse buy, such as the latest phone, a bargain on Ebay or cheap tickets to a gig.

The third bucket is the investment bucket. This bucket is used to hold all monies that are going to be used for long-term savings and invested for seven years or more on the investment markets where there is the possibility of real growth, the chance of your money making money. And the fourth bucket is the giving, or charity, bucket. This is the money you can give to family or good causes when there is another famine or tsunami.

There is a formula for this which we will cover in more detail in Chapter 5, after I have talked about bank accounts and investments. But the first thing we will consider is where money comes from. You need something to put in the buckets if my method is going to work!

KEY TAKE AWAYS

- From the dawn of time humans have used some form of currency. For a long time it was based around something of value like gold, then paper money took over. Today we are in the age where currency is becoming largely digital based.

- Money means different things to different people. For most of us, money means having the freedom to do the things we want to do.

- Your childhood experiences can make you cautious or careless—and this applies to your attitudes to money also.

- We are a debt-laden society and this can be dangerous when combined with the wealth of advertising telling you what you need.

- Spending less than you earn, equals happiness. Spending more than you earn, equals misery.

- Think of budgeting as putting money into three buckets— one for spending, one for savings and one for investing.

2 Where Does Money Come From?

Money = Work

From the day you are born to the day you leave school, your parents are responsible for putting a roof over your head, food on the table, shoes on your feet and a whole lot more. To assume everyone has two parents to meet all the expenses of raising you to be healthy, educated, and upright members of society is very limited. Families take many different shapes.

The concept of the nuclear family with mum, dad, and two children is misleading. You could be living with just one parent, with your grandparents, or in foster care. Nevertheless, an adult has the responsibility of caring for you, and they have to go to work to meet the expense unless, of course, they are one of the very few with an unearned income, a passive income, that covers a family's needs. For most of us, money equals work.

The majority of you will have been given pocket money. From an early age, you will have received a small amount of money each week to buy a comic, or a treat, and to save in your money box. You may have been encouraged to make your bed, and to help out around the home, and rewarded with pocket money as a way of establishing the work ethic; one of the most important keys to a good life.

Ever heard of 'Mr. Whippy' ice-cream? 'Mr. Whippy' made a fortune. Instead of sitting around and spending his father's money, Mr. Whippy's son is the co-founder of an upmarket chocolate firm earning a fortune in his own right. Inheriting the work ethic, Andrew Thirwell said, "You could say we've been busy. And we still are…. We've loved bringing you new ways to experience cocoa since we started out over twenty years ago – here's to the next twenty."

And, as you grow up, you may have taken on a Saturday job and opened a savings account, allowing for your increasing maturity. You could take a summer holiday job to supplement your allowance, to pay for driving lessons, or to increase your savings. Some of you may have received gifts of money for Christmas and birthdays from parents, grandparents and other relatives and have squirreled it away in your savings account, or spent it no sooner than you received it. One way or another, you will be used to handling a little money.

The average pocket money, or allowance, for a sixteen-year-old, is £10 per week. You may get more or less depending on your family's circumstance. The average cost of raising a child is £75 per week, or £4000 every year. Multiply that over time and you will quickly realise the bank of mum and dad will not last forever!

Sooner or later, the majority of you will have to stand on your own two feet, take responsibility, get a job and start handling much larger sums of money. From pocket money of around £10 per week to the minimum wage for a young worker of around £154 per week may look like a big difference, but you are going to have to make it go a long way. Earning your own money and not being reliant on anyone else is extremely satisfying. Whether you come from a happy home or can't wait to get away, becoming your own person, controlling your own spending and saving, has huge rewards.

If you are continuing your education and going to university, you will receive an annual income of nearly £16,000 made up of your student loan and grant, if you are not receiving parental support, a bursary or a scholarship. This may look like a lot of money, but it has to cover all the essentials, including rent and tuition. With tuition fees of £8,507, you are left with £144 a week; about the same as your friend who went straight to work after leaving school.

If you supplement your income by working in the long vacations, you will be much better off. As a graduate you will command a higher starting salary. Follow the **bucket list method** to manage your money, save and you can't go far wrong.

As I said, this book gives you a formula to manage your money. I am not going to do too much number crunching, or teach you how to keep your accounts, but I will give you a new way to think about your money, now and when you are in work.

Work = Money

When you reach your sixteenth birthday, you are allowed to leave school and take a job. You may already know what you want to do, or you may be trying out different jobs until you find something you really enjoy. If you are passionate about cars, you might want to be a motor mechanic, and if you love fashion, you might want a job in a clothes shop.

If you love animals, you might want to work for a local vet, and if you are a strong swimmer, you could be training as a lifeguard. Loving what you do makes it so much easier to get up each day and go to work. The more you put into your work, the more you will get out of it, both in terms of job satisfaction and the financial rewards.

The same reasoning applies to those of you going on to university or college. You may have an ambition or vocation and know exactly what you want to do and see your life all mapped out. Alternatively, you may have applied for a language course, history or math degree, because you are good at French, history or math. With no clear idea of your career choice, you are going to wait and see what happens.

It might seem to be a good idea to be fluid and leave your options open but three years of studying is a long time, and you could end up in a job you don't really want and, over your working life of forty-five years or more, never feel fulfilled or happy.

One teenager was a passionate reader and loved traveling. He prized all authors from J.K. Rowling to Ernest Hemingway. With good grades, he won a place at Cambridge University to study land management. At the last minute, he declined his place and decided to go to Newcastle University to study English literature. He knew he would never be happy working in an office. He is now a very contented teacher, passing on his love of literature to A-level students, helping them to achieve.

And he has the long school holidays to travel and see the world. He is not earning the huge salary he potentially would have been paid as a commercial estate agent, but he is happy, both at home and at work.

Whatever your choice of career or job, consider what balance of new activities you are about to discover or what familiar favourites will be the most fulfilling. You will need a good relationship with both work and money to get the most out of life.

Employed or Self-Employed?

For many, young adulthood is a time of tentatively finding your place in the world, sleeping late, partying hard and tuk-

tukking around Thailand in your gap year. 'Now' is what you might consider most important. Spare a little thought to the world of work and finding a job or career that excites you and everything else will fall into place.

Some of you will have a burning ambition to open a shop, to be an artist selling your paintings, to set up a web company, or to start your own charity; any one of the amazing entrepreneurial ideas we read about every day from Mark Zuckerberg and Facebook to Richard Branson and Virgin. Some are a great success, but others are a catastrophic failure and go down the plughole, with their founders broke and out looking for work.

If you become a doctor, a teacher, a nurse, or a train driver, you will know at the start of your career what you will earn each month, when you will get a pay rise, climbing the career ladder, and you can plan your life accordingly. It is all relatively straightforward.

If you work for an employer in the private sector, you will have an idea of what level of salary you should receive and your employer is responsible for paying your tax, national insurance contributions and your pension. If you work for a large organisation, you may feel invisible unless you do outstanding work that brings you to the attention of senior management, and you start to fast-track your career.

I am reminded of the story of a bank clerk who could have remained anonymous until someone tried to rob the bank he worked in, and he gave chase. Single handed, he managed to catch the thief, and this heroic act brought him to the attention of the senior management. Although it was strictly against the rules for any bank employee to apprehend a robber, as they might be armed with a gun, his bravery was rewarded. He was fast-tracked into a management program which eventually saw him as a personal assistant to the Chief Executive.

There are different, and less dramatic ways of catching senior management's attention. Lots of job openings in large organisations tend to be what I call 'dead men's shoes,' where your only hope of moving up the career ladder is to replace those people who have either retired, moved to another company or died along the way!

If you are working for a smaller employer, your efforts can make a real difference to the profitability of the business, and this is often recognised in the form of promotion, increased earnings and if you are lucky, a slice of the business. There has also been a trend within the information technology sector to attract bright young people into new companies, offering them lower salaries but providing share options within the business. If the business becomes successful and it is eventually sold, these share options could be worth a significant amount of money.

This type of arrangement is trying to mirror the employment strategies of the IT companies in the USA. Microsoft, Google, and Facebook have turned employees into millionaires overnight when the companies were floated on the Stock Market. There are, unfortunately, more unsuccessful start-ups than there are successful ones, so beware when trying to find the right employer with the right contract and package, or you could find yourself laid off, redundant and broke, as all your potential value was in the share options which are now worthless.

At some point in your working life, you may be faced with the choice of transitioning from being an employee to being self-employed. The very thought of jumping into a small boat, going out to sea in uncharted water fills most with fear and trepidation. Very few people leave school and become self-employed immediately.

They may go into a family business where the tradition has been to work for yourself, or they may be lucky enough to have a particular skill or talent that enables them to be a self-employed sports person, a coach or mentor, a writer, musician or an artist. A strong leader with a passion and a vision, that sets up a business to make it real, perhaps.

If you work for yourself, you not only have to produce a great product, or give a fantastic service, but you have to take care of a host of complex problems, such as marketing, sales, invoicing, and keeping accounts. And you have to pay your staff each month, and the tax man every year, before you pay yourself.

Most successful entrepreneurs have worked for a company or organisation before setting up their own business. They don't give up on their dream of being their own boss but use the experience as a training field. Nigel Botterill, the fearless bank clerk, now runs the Entrepreneurial Circle, which helps other business owners escape mediocrity and achieve more than they ever thought possible.

Far from mediocre, have you heard of Innocent, the juice company who not only make natural, delicious, healthy drinks that "help people live well and die old," but run their business in an entirely refreshing and new way? Like many such collaborations, three young men met at university and discovered they had the same aim; they wanted to be their own boss. They started Innocent after selling their smoothies at a music festival. They put up a big sign asking people if they thought they should give up their day jobs to make smoothies, and put a bin saying 'Yes' and one saying 'No' in front of the stall.

They got people to vote with their empties. The 'Yes' bin was full, so they resigned from their jobs the next day and got cracking. As a result of their enormous success, every year they hold their very own AGM, "A Grown-up Meeting," where 150 of young adults get to visit Innocent. You get to ask some questions, and learn a bit more about the business; a great way to find out if out if you have got what it takes to set up on your own.

Innocent may help 150 young people every year, but The Prince's Trust helps 56,000. They believe that every young person should have the chance to succeed and give support for starting a business. They work with 18 to 30-year-olds to turn big ideas into a business reality through their Enterprise programme. From training and mentoring support, to creating a business plan, funding, and resources, they are with you every step of the way.

Joel, 18, from Birmingham, grew up in a one bedroom flat shared with his mother and eight brothers and sisters. When he turned to The Prince's Trust, he had no idea he'd go on to be independent and working full-time. It is not just university graduates who become entrepreneurs. They help young people who are unemployed or struggling at school, to transform their lives.

The internet presents a great opportunity for young people, in particular, to set up businesses, as young people are the best at social media and technology.

You spend most of your time on the internet, and so can create businesses better than the older generation when it comes to these areas.

A mentor can be a huge help in overcoming some of the difficulties you will face creating a business for the first time, so don't be afraid to ask people for help. They will probably be quite flattered that you came to them.

Unearned income

As I said, work equals money, but there are other forms of income you don't work for; unearned or passive income. You could say, "Wow, I want some of that," but whatever the source of your money, your income, it comes with a great responsibility. You will still have to know how to look after your money, see you are paying the correct amount of tax, and it is invested wisely to take care of you and, in time, your family.

Disability Benefits

Not all things are equal. Life is not a level playing field. Some of you might be disabled, unable to go to work and be receiving state benefits to cover your all your living costs and to help you to become independent. This is still your income. You deserve it and you need to look after it in the same way as your friends need to manage their wages or salary.

Trust Fund

From one extreme to another, a few of you may have a trust fund, money set aside by, or inherited from, a wealthy parent or grandparent, for your benefit. It will either give you an income, paid into your account at regular intervals, or a lump sum at say, the age of 25. It might be a small amount of money, to supplement your earned income, or a large sum of money which means you never have to work. If it is invested wisely, you will be able to enjoy the income and pass on the capital, the sum invested, to your own children one day.

Interest Payments

If you have a savings account, it will be earning interest, day by day and year by year. Interest rates are currently very low which doesn't inspire savers, but your money is working for you. This is your passive income. You will need your money to work harder if you are going to get your assets, your wealth, to grow but we will come to that later.

Stocks & Shares

If you have money invested in stocks and shares, this gives rise to a particular set of problems; one day you could be rich, and the next the bottom has fallen out of the market, making grown men cry. Stocks, shares, and equities are all words used to describe what is essentially the same thing.

When you buy a share, you are buying ownership of part of a company, and you become a shareholder in that company. You are investing your money in that company by buying an equity stake. The value of your share can change and, as an investor, your objective is to sell your share for a higher price than you paid for it. The profit you make when you sell is your passive income.

Property

If you own a house, flat or commercial property, and you let it out, you receive the monthly rent. A passive income. It can also create the possibility of an increase in value if, or when, you decide to sell. More unearned money called capital gains. You have the income from rent and the profit from the sale. However, it should always be remembered that property is perhaps the most illiquid of all assets, as it cannot quickly be sold or exchanged for cash without a substantial loss in value.

 **KEY TAKEAWAYS**

- Generally speaking money comes from work. It is the result of your labour. You work—you receive money.

- A good way of learning about money is to become involved early. So think about getting an after school job.

- Working for an employer gives you security, and many aspects such as tax are taken care of for you.

- A riskier option is self-employment, but equally the rewards can be greater. Mark Zuckerberg probably wouldn't be where he is today without taking risks.

- Other methods for getting money include disability allowances, trust funds, interest, shares and property investments.

3 How Do You Access & Manage Your Money?

I am not about to assume you all hold a savings account and a current account with a bank or building society but, as soon as you go to work, or to university, you are going to need one. The majority of employers, both small businesses and large organisations, will need your bank details to pay you every week or month, as they transfer your wages or salary directly into your current account.

From the age of 11, you can have a savings account and current account with a cashpoint card or Visa debit card linked to an account you administer yourself. Some banks set a limit as to how much you can withdraw or spend without a grown-up's approval. You have to be 18 or over to open a full-service account with checking facilities, but students between the ages of 16 to 25 can open a Student Checking Account.

Writing a cheque to pay your rent or pay your utility bills was once standard practice. In the modern world of internet banking, cheque books have become dinosaurs, superseded by the ability to pay in shops with a debit card, and pay bills and make transfers online. At the moment, cheques take up to five days to clear your account. A new process is to be introduced across the UK banking industry where a digital image is created from the original paper cheque and, allowing for faster clearance, the funds will be made available the next working day.

In the digital world, you will be asked for your bank details in order for your wages, salary or payment for goods or services can be transferred to your account. To open an account, if you haven't already, you can visit a bank in your nearest town or go online. All you need is a recognised form of ID, such as a passport, birth certificate, adoption certificate or EU Identity Card. You will also need proof of your address.

Banks are rivals, vying for your business, and offer teenagers lots of incentives from a personalised debit card you design yourself to money off driving lessons. After all, the banks want your trade for life! But more importantly, you need to look at what rates of interest they will pay you, what charges, if any, they will make, penalties for becoming overdrawn and the bank's 'Terms and Conditions' to see you are getting the best deal before you sign your contract.

We live in a time of terms and conditions. Never before have we signed or agreed so many. With some contracts running the length of a book, written in a style so tedious that your eyeballs splinter as your brain tries to sneak out of your ears, the majority of people admit they never read them, let alone understand them. Tiny rules shape our reality; one press on your keyboard and you've accepted the ever-changing, ever-mystifying terms of Instagram and Facebook.

The issue only comes to light when things go wrong. For instance, when you crash your moped in Sri Lanka on your gap year trip and discover your travel insurance doesn't cover you. Or you send for a 'free' bottle of moisturiser, only to find it costs you a staggering £80 a month, every month because you had to give your bank details to receive the sample, and agreed to some small print that says you give permission to be billed monthly unless you opt out in time You had no idea you had agreed to the terms and conditions until you saw the money leak out of your account. The best rule-of-thumb is large print gives, small print takes away.

When you open your first bank account, it is a good idea to have two: a spending account for your daily needs, and a savings account where you can get a higher rate of interest. Research what the different banks offer online and don't be taken in by tempting, glittery special offers. After all, if you did a paper round and the newsagent offered to pay you with a free magazine instead of cash, you would say, "No way."

One more thing to consider before you decide on which bank, or building society and which account you want, are your ethics. In an increasingly diverse world, with an awareness of different cultures and beliefs, you may want a bank which does not invest in something you oppose. If environmental issues and damage to the planet are a particular concern to you, the bank you choose should not invest in environmentally damaging activities. Ask the bank before you commit what their policies are.

All UK-regulated current or savings accounts and cash ISAs in banks and building societies are covered by the Financial Services Compensation Scheme, FSCS up to £75,000. But this doesn't mean you'll get the full amount for every account if they go broke. The £75,000 is per institution. If the time comes that you have more than this in savings, invest in two separate banks that are not owned by the same organisation.

Jargon Buster

Current Account - A current account is probably the busiest account you will have, as it enables you to make all the day-to-day banking transactions that you need to. You can pay in money whenever you want. You can have a cash card and access your money at an ATM, or you can have a Visa or Mastercard Debit Card which allows you to withdraw cash and pay in shops.

You can keep a check on your account online, or by paper statement.

Whichever method you select, you need to balance the credit and debit, in and out, columns frequently to see nothing has been taken in error, and you have enough money left to cover all the expenses you plan on making.

Most parents or guardians like to keep an eye on how you are managing your money. Aside from the youth accounts offered by the high-street players, there are a growing number of other schemes and products. Osper is a service aimed at teenagers, and their parents, that consists of a prepaid MasterCard debit card and a mobile banking app. Parents load money onto their child's Osper card account, with the app enabling them to monitor transactions. There is also goHenry, aimed at the same age group, which comes with a prepaid Visa card and an app.

When you are 18, you can set up standing orders and direct debits to cover any monthly expenses, such as your mortgage or rent, utility bills, council tax, and any other regular outgoings. You set up a standing order and choose the amount and frequency, and can change or cancel it at any time.

In contrast, if you set up a direct debit to pay your electricity bill or broadband supplier, they decide how much and how often they collect the money from your current account, and they can vary the amount and frequency of collections without further permission from you.

And at 18, you can arrange an overdraft facility. If you withdraw more money than you have in your bank account, the extra money you take out after your bank balance reaches zero is called an overdraft. You should always agree on this in advance with your bank, as fees for unauthorised borrowing are much higher than for authorised overdrafts. Overdrafts are designed to help in the short term and are not meant to be a long-term loan. They can cost an arm and a leg if mismanaged.

Instant Access Savings Account - Instant access savings accounts do what they say on the tin; they allow you to withdraw your money quickly and easily.

The simple money lesson for teenagers is put your cash in the bank, and it will grow. As you get older, there's another valuable lesson to be learned. A bank's job is to make money from you. This may sound like a tough message, but it's crucially important. You can earn up to 6% if you can save £10 a month, every month, yet many people have cash in accounts paying miserable amounts. That doesn't just deprive you of interest, but the chance to learn the valuable lesson that your money can work for you.

Yours savings account is your most important account but not all of you have £10 a month to save. As early as possible, even before you consider leaving home, or go to university, the golden rule is to take your age, halve it and save that percentage of your income. Each year, on your birthday, do the sum again. Every year, just as your age and income increases, so will your savings. By the time you reach the age of thirty and can afford to put away a 15% of what you earn, the habit will be deeply embedded in your psyche.

For example, if you are 16 and have £10 per week, put away 80p every week. It doesn't sound like much, the cost of a can of Coca-Cola, but it will soon add up, especially if you leave your savings alone and add the compound interest. I will explain compound interest later.

If you are 16 and already have your first job, or are going on to college, you should be looking to save 9% of your income. Even if you are on the minimum wage of £154, with careful management you should be able to add to your savings account.

18 years old - Savings of 9% - Income £154.   154 divided by 100 [answer = 1%] x 9 = £13.86 per week or £720.72 per year. After two years you could afford to buy your first car.
Now it's starting to look more exciting. After all, if you walk past Costa or Starbucks every day and buy a latte on your way to work, or between lectures, you are going to be spending the same amount as you need to put in your savings account each week!

So let's look at interest rates. Let's assume you are 16 years-old, and you are putting away 80p every week in your savings account. You have been offered an interest rate of around 3% AER. AER stands for the Annual Equivalent Rate. It lets you compare interest rates across accounts and reflects not just the amount of interest but also how often it is paid.

The higher the AER, the greater the return. For example, two accounts advertise they pay 3 per cent a year, but one credits all the interest at the end of the year, and the other pays you 1.5 percent every six months. It may on the face of it look the same, but you will earn more money from the account which pays you every six months. The more money you save, the more interest you can shop around for.

If you leave your money to grow you will earn compound interest. Compound interest is the interest on interest. It is the result of reinvesting your interest, rather than taking what you've earned out of your account. Interest is then paid on the principal amount plus the added interest. More money for you!

Notice Savings Account - To get the best rates for your savings, it is vital you keep an eye on how much interest your money is earning. Notice Savings Accounts work in a different way to instant access deals. Instead of having quick access to your money when it suits you, saving in a notice account means you'll have to tell your bank in advance that you want to make a withdrawal. Notice accounts tend to pay more interest but impose a penalty for immediate withdrawal of any funds, usually in the form of a loss of interest.

Managing your savings account by post or via the Internet you can get an even better rate as this cuts out the need to go to a high-street branch to conduct transactions. Many of the smaller banks and building societies operate by post and internet access and offer accounts with better interest rates than the larger banks and building societies.

Fixed Term Savings Account - Fixed-rate bonds are savings accounts that offer a fixed interest rate on your cash for a set period. While they often come with higher interest rates, opening a fixed term savings account will mean giving up access to your money during the term of the bond.

Fixed-rate bonds can extend over one year, two years; even three, four or five years. The longer you're prepared to lock your money away, the higher your return will be. While it may be possible to get your money out of a fixed-rate bond in an emergency, you stand to pay a hefty penalty for doing so. Tying up your cash in a fixed-rate bond is only a good idea if you're confident you won't need to get at it.

'Help to Save' accounts will be launched within the next two years, offering low-paid workers a government bonus of up to £1,200. Workers receiving universal credit will be able to save a maximum of £50 a month and receive a 50% bonus after two years, worth up to £600. They can then choose to save for another two years, with a further £600 bonus available. In total, account holders can build a pot of £3,600 over four years, with a £1,200 contribution from the government.

Withdrawals will be allowed to cover 'urgent costs' and there will be no restrictions on how savings can be used at the end of the term. The government has yet to decide on how this savings scheme will be implemented, but it should be available no later than April 2018.

Post Office Accounts were once widespread, especially in rural areas as it was easier to conduct your banking business through the Post Office than it was to go into the nearest town. The Post Office has now has been taken over by the Bank of Ireland and is effectively just another bank.

Guaranteed Equity Bonds, GEBs, are invested in a number of stocks, but run for a set period and usually promise to return the initial amount invested, plus a set amount of growth.

National Savings Bonds - are one of the few sources of index-linked savings offering two, three, and five-year certificates. This is a good way of keeping pace with inflation but with inflation currently less than 1%, the returns for these are not spectacular but are a hedge for future inflation increases. A hedge fund is an investment fund that pools capital from a limited number of sources and invests in a variety of assets. In effect, the government is borrowing your money to invest.

Premium Bonds are backed by HM Treasury so you never lose your capital. They're a savings account where the interest earned is decided by a monthly prize draw. Each £1 buys a bond entered into the draw, and any winnings are tax-free.

The minimum you can invest is £100, the maximum £30,000. Every bond stands an equal chance of winning thanks to Ernie, the Electronic Random Number Indicator Equipment. You can choose to have winnings automatically reinvested into more bonds, up to the maximum of £30,000 but the odds of winning the top prize for each bond are 1 in 47 billion. A lottery ticket has odds of 1 in 14 million for the jackpot. Both are a gamble so you could be far better off investing your money in an ISA.

ISA Account is an individual savings account, a scheme allowing individuals to hold cash, shares, and unit trusts without paying tax on the interest or on the investment returns you receive. To open an ISA, you need to be a UK resident for tax purposes and aged 16 or over. For some ISAs, you may need to be 18 or over.

For this tax year, the total ISA allowance per adult is £11,280. You can only put up to £5,640 of this amount into a cash ISA. The remaining £5,640 will have to be invested in equity or stocks and shares ISAs. According to HMRC, 72% of ISA accounts are invested in cash but in the long term, the real value will be steadily depleted by the impact of inflation. In contrast, these past three years have seen extraordinarily strong returns on developed world stock markets.

ISAs are an ideal method of holding smaller amounts of money, especially when those savings are made on a regular monthly basis, as the interest can be paid with no tax deducted, subject to certain rules and regulations.

Jisas, Junior ISAs, allow parents or grandparents to invest up to £4,000 a year in cash, stocks or funds. The accounts are in a child's name, and the returns can only be accessed once the child is 18 and are paid free of income or capital gains tax. A great way for parents to put money away for your education, if they can afford to.

Tax – Unlike ISAs, one thing you need to cater for on any payment of interest from a bank or building society is taxation. Following the introduction of the personal savings allowance in April 2016, banks no longer deduct income tax from the interest they pay you on your account. You are now responsible for paying any tax due to HM Revenue and Customs.

Property - Buy-to-let properties are for those people who can afford to put high deposits down for buying a property or can buy a property outright. Many lenders insist that instead of paying an interest-only loan, part of the capital has to be repaid each month to the lender. Most of the flats or houses or you will rent when you first leave home, or go to university are buy-to-let investments.

Property, as an asset class, is when you invest in directly held property funds or in real-estate investment trusts, REITS, owning the property as part of a group of investors, through a pension fund, for example.

Stocks and Shares. In financial markets, a share is a unit of account for various investments. The stock is an ownership share in a corporation, like Apple or Google, but is also used for collective investments such as real estate investment trusts. Each of these shares denotes a part ownership. Stocks are traded on exchanges all over the world.

There are 2,000 funds available to UK investors and correctly identifying the ones that will do well at any given time can be difficult. If you have a few thousand pounds to invest, you could spread your money by putting equal amounts into low, medium and high-risk funds.

Another option for a beginner is the tracker, the FTSE 100, which follows the movements of stocks and shares. Footsie is the nickname for the Financial Times Stock Exchange Index, which includes the 100 largest publicly owned stocks listed on the London Stock Exchange. Dow Jones is the equivalent in the U.S. Before you get started, ask an expert.

Financial Advisers are the experts. If you are looking to invest, buy a financial product or plan for the longer term, you may need financial advice depending on how complicated your finances and personal circumstances are, and your short and long- term goals.

Wealth Managers - Wealth management is a high-level professional service that combines financial and investment advice, accounting and tax services, retirement planning and legal and estate planning.

Psychology of investing – take a risk or play it safe?

When it comes to investments, you might need some help before making speculations which see real growth in your capital and unearned income, especially when it comes to pension planning. A competent financial adviser will find out what kind of saver and investor you are before giving advice. Proper psychometric risk profiling establishes whether or not you have a capacity for risk.

Psychometric risk profiling is a set of questions designed to assess your tolerance for risk. Some people show a greater capacity to jeopardise their wealth and walk away from any loss saying, "It's only money," while even a small loss would make others lose sleep at night or become sick with depression. It is like asking someone at the funfair if they have a head for heights or if they suffer from vertigo before riding the roller-coaster.

The worst case is always for the individual who thinks they have a capacity for risk only to find out too late they are devastated by any loss. Getting a piece of the stock market action can be tempting for rookie investors. Tales of other people's gains can make you wonder why your savings are in a safe account when you could be buying into a share of the action that could help your money grow much faster.

The first question to ask yourself before investing in the stock market is how much money do you have to invest? The second question, how you would feel if you initially lost money? And the third question, can you afford to take a risk?

Another golden rule is to leave your investment alone for the medium term; at least three and preferably five years or more. A stock market investment needs time to develop, and huge gains in short periods are unlikely.

Once your risk-tolerance is established, you can allocate a certain amount of either your lump sum or monthly savings to various asset classes. There are only really four asset classes, and all others are a variation or combination of these. They are cash, property, bonds, and stocks and shares.

The 'father' of asset allocation was Professor Harry Markowitz, an American academic, who put together his efficient portfolio theory, for which he won a Nobel Prize. A portfolio is your collection investments. The basis of Markowitz's theory was the majority of all investment performance is about the original asset allocation and little of the growth of an investment portfolio is down to market timing or, indeed, an individual's skill. He also noted that it was possible to lower the risk by blending the mix of assets to suit an individual's risk profile.

A low risk-taker should have most of their investment portfolio in bonds, and less in stocks, whereas a high-risk taker should put more into stocks and shares and less in bonds. It would further reduce the risk to put some property into the mix. An investment portfolio also requires a little cash to 'oil the wheels,' to pay the fees of running the portfolio.

The golden rule, once you have decided on an asset allocation is to stick with it through thick and thin, as this will be your guide to performance over the long term.

Your generation are going to have to work harder for longer than previous generations. The state pension age is now 65. Many of you will start to work soon and by the time you retire the pension age will have risen dramatically. If you build up your savings from an early age, you will not have to fear abject poverty in old age.

When it comes to finances there is a lot to take on board. Life is not a fairytale, and I can't tell you the secret of 'happy ever after'. No one can predict what will happen along the way; your journey is just beginning. What I can tell you is, if you watch your back and look after your money from a young age, you too can have some savings, a portfolio and the chance of a better life.

 **KEY TAKEAWAYS**

- Save your cash and it will grow.

- Part of this involves getting a bank account. If you don't have one yet—you'll need one as soon as you begin work.

- It's a good idea to have a chequing/spending account as well as a higher interest savings/investment account.

- Thinking about sharemarket investments? Firstly, decide if you are a risk taker, or risk adverse. Think about how much you have to invest, and if you can afford to lose it? If you can't—then think twice.

4 Money Mindset

It's not about how much money you have to spend, but how you spend it that matters. The ability to control money and save money requires discipline and self-awareness; a healthy mindset and a healthy savings account. The same discipline you have to put into keeping fit or playing a musical instrument. Let things slide, and you get out of shape.

It is common sense you cannot live like a millionaire unless you have the income of a millionaire and yet so many people are in debt; a debt they can't sustain. To understand the fundamental rule - you cannot spend more than you earn without causing yourself misery - does not require huge intelligence and yet many people who left school without a single exam pass are now millionaires, whereas some who attained honours degrees are hugely in debt. If you master your money, you will have more of it and it will work for you, rather than against you.

With the financial press full of headlines about feckless millennials who would rather bandy their minimal cash around than put it in a savings account, it's easy to unfairly write off the younger generation as irresponsible. There are a lot of negative stereotypes about teenagers. Teenagers are habitually criticised for being obsessed with technology, apathetic about politics, shirking responsibility, spending all their money on drugs and drink and generally being careless. Such views are inaccurate and overblown. The data is striking. In Great Britain:

- Those aged under 25 are a third more likely to be teetotal now than in 2005

- A quarter of young people do not drink at all

- Illegal drug use among the under-25s has also fallen by more than a quarter since 2004

- The number of nightclubs has almost halved since 2005

- Teenage pregnancy is at its lowest since records began in England and Wales in 1969

- The number of crimes committed by under-18s in England and Wales has fallen by 70% since 2005, to a new record low, according to the Office of National Statistics

The image of the young as a generation personified by their drunken escapades in Ibiza is in need of revisiting! You were born into a time of plenty but have grown up in the worst recession the West has seen; the consequence of previous generations being greedy and feckless, morally and financially bankrupt. Consumers and bankers alike joined in the collective delusion that lasting prosperity could be built on ever-bigger piles of debt, borrowing more than they could realistically afford.

We start with the folly of the bankers. The years before the crisis saw a flood of irresponsible mortgage lending. Loans were doled out to 'subprime' borrowers with poor credit histories who struggled to repay them. These risky mortgages were passed on to financial engineers at the big banks where the long period of economic stability over which bankers preside encouraged risk-taking.

In August 2007, Northern Rock was first major UK bank to acknowledge the risk of exposure to subprime mortgage markets. They had borrowed large sums of money for customers, and needed to pay off its debt by re-selling those mortgages in the international capital markets. But demand had fallen and Northern Rock faced a liquidity crisis and needed a loan from the British government.

This sparked fears the bank would go bankrupt, prompting the first run on a bank for 150 years, as customers to queued round the block to withdraw their savings. Adam Applegarth, Northern Rock's chief executive, later said that it was, "the day the world changed." It marked the cut-off point between 'an Edwardian summer' of prosperity and tranquility and the trench warfare of the credit crunch; the failed banks, the petrified markets, the property markets blown to pieces by a shortage of credit.

The collapse of Lehman Brothers, a sprawling global bank, almost brought down the world's financial system. It took huge taxpayer-financed bailouts to shore up the banking industry. Even so, the ensuing credit crunch turned what was already a nasty downturn into the worst recession in 80 years.

Massive monetary and fiscal stimulus prevented a depression, but the effects of the crash are still rippling through the world economy. Thousands lost their jobs and their homes all because of a bunch of short-selling spivs and speculators in the financial markets loaning money to the people who could least afford it and the banks turning a blind eye.

Identified by economist and futures analyst Noreena Hertz, an honorary professor at University College London, as being a part of a new, "hyper-aware and supremely anxious generation," teenagers today are more mature, more ambitious, more terrified of debt, redundancy, homelessness and the state of the planet than their predecessors.

With the world's news of terrorist attacks, famine, disaster and the state of the economy constantly relayed into your smartphones, via Twitter and Facebook, it is hardly surprising your fears stretch way beyond the typical teenage anxieties of exams, boyfriends, and girlfriends.

Teenagers are now nicknamed Generation K: the K standing for Katniss Everdeen, the spirited heroine of the book series and film franchise The Hunger Games, which tells the troubling story of life in a harsh, bombed-out, Big Brother society. Hertz conducted interviews with 16-18 year-olds. Her research revealed, "They're actually a very surprisingly financially cautious generation. This isn't the irresponsible teenagers of yore, they're more likely to save as a precaution than the next couple of generations up. They're putting their babysitting money and their odd job money into their savings."[1]

While you are very much 'tech heads' you are also aware of the potential dangers that new technology brings. You deliberately chose to use cash, openly saying that with cash you feel you know what you are spending, whereas with plastic it's so hard to stay in control. Hertz asked one teenage focus group to imagine a technology product or app that would be most useful to them in their financial decision-making. They identified an app which, each time they were going to buy something, sent a message which said, "Do you really need this?"

A new bank is trying to adopt this futuristic concept. Simply named 'B,' this bank is built around an app for tablets and

1 http://www.noreena.com/generation-k-why-todays-teens-are-more-careful-with-their-money/

smartphones. 'B' is an intuitive app with a range of interactive tools designed to help you stay in control of your money. By analysing your spending, 'B' can see where you might have extra cash left in any month, or let you know your finances might be a little tight.

Along with the ability to set up savings pots, tag, and track spending or automatically sweep cash between current and savings accounts, 'B' will tell you whether you're good to go when you want a new pair of trainers, or stop you in your tracks when you want a new guitar.

Staying with the analogy of the Hunger Games and Generation K, the protagonist Katniss is resourceful, mature, responsible and rebellious. She has a rational sense of what is right and fair, and a high tolerance for risk; skills developed with the challenge of growing up in one of the poorest of the 12 districts of Panem.

There are nine main cognitive biases, or personality traits, which can prevent you from being rational and determine whether you will end up comfortably well-off or whether you will end up poor. Likewise, there are a number of positive personality traits that people who are well-off possess, and people who are poor do not.

Take a look at the scorecard below to find out how your mindset will affect your financial decision-making:

Exercise: The Money Mindset Scorecard

ANXIETY
Anxiety influences an investor's emotional engagement in the short term, and the extent to which they allow reactions to the ups and downs of financial markets to undermine their long-term financial objectives. The value of stocks and shares can change every day and expose some to panic sell, as if under attack from tracker jackers, the mutant wasps in Panem.

NOT AT ALL		ALL THE TIME

BANDWAGON EFFECT
Bandwagon Effect. We are influenced the collective thoughts and the behaviour of those around us. Jumping on the bandwagon, the 'herd' influence is the tendency for investors to irrationally follow the decisions of others because they fear they might be missing out. No doubt you see this in school everyday. It takes just one admired individual to wear something original and by the next week the entire school has the same outfit. If you look at what others are doing and irrationally follow their decision, your are one of the herd. Be an individual at all costs.

NOT AT ALL		ALL THE TIME

PROJECTION BIAS

Projection bias is a tendency to project your current feelings onto a future event. This is when people try to foresee their future and often make mistakes, forgetting that they will probably feel differently when the future becomes the present. We can recognise this bias in Peeta who didn't believe he had any of the skills he would need to even compete in the Hunger Games.

NOT AT ALL		**ALL THE TIME**

IRRATIONAL PERCEPTION

Irrational Perception. Most people don't have a rational picture of their wealth and income. You will recognise this bias if you don't understand the difference between supposed wealth and real income and wealth. You may also not fully appreciate the power of compound interest and the effect of inflation on real returns.

NOT AT ALL		**ALL THE TIME**

AVERSION

Aversion. An investor with loss aversion tends to feel the lows of a loss more than the highs of a gain, which can make the ups and downs of risky investments an emotional tug of war.

NOT AT ALL		**ALL THE TIME**

PRESENT BIAS

Present Bias. As a general rule, humans care more about the present than the future; it's the year of Now, and some of you don't want to think any further. Given two similar rewards, humans prefer the one that arrives sooner rather than later, and this present bias explains why so many investors find it so difficult to save sufficiently for the future.

NOT AT ALL | | **ALL THE TIME**

OVER-OPTIMISM

Over-optimism. Overestimating success and underestimating risk is called over-optimism, which can result in poor decisions and over-exposure to risk. You can recognise this bias if you tend to be unrealistic about the future, have an inability to think ahead, and often procrastinate instead of taking preventative action

NOT AT ALL | | **ALL THE TIME**

INVESTOR LITERACY

Investor Literacy. The extent of your knowledge about investments will have a significant impact on your financial outcomes. It is not the case that those with knowledge always do better, but those with lower investor literacy should consider focusing on simpler, easy-to-understand financial products, and place greater importance on the advice of others who are more experienced.

NOT AT ALL | | **ALL THE TIME**

OVERCONFIDENCE BIAS

Overconfidence Bias. This is a tendency to believe in yourself without giving due consideration to chance, external events or alternative options. This is a dangerous bias because it can lead to decisions based on opinion rather than fact. Like the tributes from the more prosperous districts of Panem, this bias can create arrogance. The overconfident tend to ignore the possible impact of chance and events outside of their control. They tend to take credit for all achievements and successes but blame others for their failures. They may also accept more risk than is perhaps necessary, and keep changing their mind instead of sticking to a long-term plan.

NOT AT ALL		ALL THE TIME

HELPFUL

Helpful. How much of your valuable time do you lose parked in front of a screen? Two-thirds of wealthy people watch less than an hour of TV a day, and spend less than an hour a day on the Internet unless it is job-related. Instead, these successful people use their free time engaged in personal development, networking, volunteering, or pursuing some goal that will lead to rewards down the road. Almost three-quarters of wealthy people network and volunteer a minimum of five hours a month. Katniss has a deep compassion for others, and thrives on taking care of the helpless.

NOT AT ALL		ALL THE TIME

CONFIDENCE

Confidence. Anxiety is perhaps the most important negative emotion to control. Any change, even positive changes, can prompt feelings of fear. Wealthy people have conditioned their minds to overcome these thoughts, while those who struggle give in to fear and allow it to hold them back. Whether you fear change, making mistakes, taking risks or simply failure, conquering these emotions is about building confidence.

NOT AT ALL   **ALL THE TIME**

POSITIVE

Positive. Almost four out of five wealthy people attribute their success in life to their beliefs. Successful people create their own unique type of good luck. Their positive habits lead to opportunities such as promotions, bonuses, new business and good health.

NOT AT ALL   **ALL THE TIME**

ATTENTIVE

Attentive. You should listen to others five minutes for every one minute that you speak. Wealthy people are good communicators because they are good listeners. They understand that you can learn and educate yourself only by listening to what other people have to say.

NOT AT ALL   **ALL THE TIME**

REALISTIC

Realistic. You cannot control the outcome of a wish, but you can control the outcome of a goal. Every year, you should pursue at least one major goal.

NOT AT ALL		ALL THE TIME

UNIQUE

Unique. An individual takes their own council or the advice of a reliable mentor. They don't jump on the bandwagon and follow the herd but create their own style.

NOT AT ALL		ALL THE TIME

CREATIVE

Creative. People who pursue a dream or a main purpose in life are by far the wealthiest and happiest among us. Because they love what they do for a living, they are happy to devote more hours each day driving toward their purpose.

NOT AT ALL		ALL THE TIME

RESPONSIBLE

Responsible. Wealthy people avoid overspending. They pay their future selves first by saving.

NOT AT ALL		ALL THE TIME

OBJECTIVE

Objective. Not every thought needs to come out of your mouth. Not every emotion needs to be expressed. When you say whatever is on your mind, you risk hurting others. Wealthy people filter their emotions. They understand that letting emotions control them can destroy relationships at work and at home. Wait to say what's on your mind until you are calm and have had time to look at the situation objectively.

NOT AT ALL		ALL THE TIME

INFORMED

Informed. Reading information that will increase your knowledge about your business or career will make you more valuable to colleagues, customers or clients. The majority of wealthy people read 30 minutes or more every day. By increasing their knowledge, they are able to see more opportunities and understand their investments.

NOT AT ALL		ALL THE TIME

Everyone has these characteristics, no matter how clever or financially literate they are. These are mental traps that occur in all aspects of life. The good news is that once you are aware of the biases you can think more rationally about your decisions and avoid the pitfalls, build up your confidence concentrating on your positive traits.

It is hardly surprising most teenagers are hyper-aware, supremely anxious and terrified of debt. Even though the economy has improved, following the 2008 collapse, money worries are still the most significant source of stress for adults, ranking higher than work, family responsibilities, and health problems. The stress that debt causes invades every aspect of life, work, home, personal relationships, and your hopes for the future. Many of you will have witnessed arguments over money, sometimes resulting in a traumatic divorce and a disrupted, unhappy family life.

The close links between money, well-being, and poverty are commonly known to be a potent and toxic stressor. Nobel

Prize winner psychologist, Daniel Kahneman, said that *more* money does not necessarily buy happiness, but *less* money is associated with emotional pain. For millions living in the grip of financial pressure, the issue is *less* about being below poverty lines and far more to do with money habits and practices that are not sustainable economically, socially, environmentally or spiritually.

There's a form of debt that is of paramount concern to teenagers; student loans. You are constantly told that only a university education can give you a decent future. And then you're told that, to pay for it, you need to go into debt. Before you even step on the career ladder, you are saddled with debt and enslaved to the government, who loaned you the money.

In the past, education was about teaching people something. Now, it is also about making sure teenagers develop a reliable compass, the navigational skills and the character qualities that will help you find your way through an uncertain, volatile and ambiguous world. I am encouraging you to take control, save and avoid owing money but on the other hand, you are told that if you want an education, you will have to contend with debt for years to come.

Needless to say, students with their sights set on university are being put off for all the wrong reasons. Although student debt is unwelcome, it's still important that students go to university and fulfill their ambitions. It's more important than ever for young people to know the facts before possibly turning down a life changing experience.

To stay in control, you will need to appreciate different ideas, perspectives and values. Whether you have the ambition to become a high-flyer or to live off-grid, build your own house and grow your own food, you are going to need to adjust your thoughts, feelings and behaviours. You will need to think critically and scrutinise your expenditure if you are to avoid debt, or limit the damage and sidestep anxiety and stress.

Hope is a stronger emotion than fear. No greater example of this can be found in the story of J.K. Rowling, the wealthy author and generous philanthropist who created Harry Potter. When she was writing the first Harry Potter book, she was a single mother bringing up her daughter on benefits. She said that she had to count every penny to make sure it lasted the week as they were so poor, "As poor as it is possible to be in Britain without being homeless." There were times when she wondered whether they would actually make it through to the end of the week before she got her next benefit payment. When invited to give an address at Harvard University, she said to an enthralled audience of graduates, "The knowledge that you have emerged wiser and stronger from setbacks means you are, ever after, secure in your ability to survive."

Student Loans

If you are one of the many students who go onto further education, whether university or college, you will be offered the chance to pay any tuition fees and other costs with a student loan. The main body for giving student loans in the UK is The Student Loans Company, the SLC, which is a Government-funded business. A student loan can be given to anyone in full-time higher education and covers tuition fees, maintenance fees, and any grants for living costs.

Some of you will have parents who have set aside savings for your education to help you avoid a student loan but, for the majority, the bank of mum and dad may not extend this far. A million students each year need a student loan.

You may be eligible for a tuition fee grant which is a non-repayable Government grant but, in most cases, a tuition fee loan is made to cover university or college costs. The maintenance loan is for living costs and there are varying rates you are entitled to, depending on where you are studying and where you live; whether you live at home or have moved away.

There are additional loans for students studying in London, to allow for higher costs of living. The maintenance loans are paid directly into your bank account at the start of each term, monthly for students in Scotland, and the tuition fees paid directly to your college or university.

The method of repayment depends on your circumstances. If you are employed, repayments will be deducted at source by your employer through Pay As You Earn [PAYE] at 15% of your monthly income once you earn over £21,000[1]. If you are self-employed, repayments will be calculated through a Self Assessment tax return.

Re-payers are identified in the UK Tax System by their National Insurance Number. This is provided when you first apply for a student loan. The SLC instructs HM Revenue & Customs to notify you, or your employer, when repayments are due to start. Repayments are deducted from taxable earnings and allocated to your loan account balance annually. When the balance is expected to be fully repaid, HMRC notifies you or your employer that repayments should cease.

---

1 Source: www.studentloanrepayment.co.uk as of 15th June 2016

The criteria where your student loan is automatically canceled depends on when and where you took out your first student loan. In England or Wales, your student loan is canceled 30 years after you become eligible to repay and in Scotland, 35 years. If a borrower can prove they're permanently unfit for work due to a disability, then their loan could be written off.

You start repaying your student loan when your income reaches £21,000[2] per year. If you are earning £25,000, your monthly repayments will be £30 rising to £217 per month at £50,000

per annum. Currently, the headline interest rate is 3%, plus the Retail Price Index, RPI, or put simply, 3.9%

As soon as you graduate, alongside your degree, you could be in debt to the tune of £44,000. This means, as a newly-recruited professional worker, you could be paying for university well into your 50s. Student loans can be a burden on an individual for many years and should, therefore, be treated with extreme caution before entering into such an agreement. You will not be able to escape the debt even if you move abroad.

With this in mind you can avoid student loan debt, or at least make it more bearable, if you save your money as early on

2 Source: www.studentloanrepayment.co.uk as of 15th June 2016

as possible, get as many scholarships as you can, become an intern, get a grant, find part-time work and holiday work. Those of you who come from a household with a combined income of less than £42,611 a year can apply for extra funding in the form of a maintenance grant.

When it comes to scholarships, universities want students who will excel academically, and who will represent the university positively when they enter the workplace. Companies also want to offer bright, underprivileged students the opportunity to succeed. Look into available academic scholarships, and take advantage of them. In addition to academic brilliance, some scholarships recognise students who demonstrate specific core values and principles. Students who volunteer, or who demonstrate strong leadership qualities, may be eligible for these types of scholarship opportunities.

With hard work, perseverance, ingenuity, and imagination you can diminish your student loan debt. Borrow less, spend less and create a supplemental income. That way, you can graduate from college without having to worry about being completely broke.

Other Loans

We have talked at great length about student loans, but many of you will be going straight from school into the workplace. The first time you need a loan might be to furnish a rented property when you leave home, or to buy a car and you approach your bank to see what rates they are offering. Don't forget to shop around, as your own bank might not have the best offer.

When you want a loan, or a credit card, you will come across three little letters. APR stands for Annual Percentage Rate. Presented as a percentage, APR is a calculation of the full amount you will pay for a loan over the course of one year. The calculation includes any fees you may need to pay, plus the interest rate a lender applies. In a nutshell, APR is a percentage which tells consumers how much it will cost to borrow money. The higher the APR, the more you will pay.

APR is a very prominent figure within financial services because it is used widely by lenders. Every lender calculates it in the same way. As it is a standard measurement, it is considered to be a useful figure which can help consumers compare and contrast different financial products. All lenders have a legal obligation to give an accurate APR before their customers take on a loan.

Representative and typical APR are two different ways of working out and presenting APR. While every lender uses the same calculation, there are a few variables which may make APR seem higher or lower on paper. This is because different consumers will qualify for different rates and may incur different fees and charges.

When lenders use the expression 'representative APR,' they are referring to a rate which 51% or more of applicants for their product will be offered. This rate includes all interest, fees and compulsory extras, including things like obligatory insurance policies.

When lenders advertise a 'typical APR,' they are referring to a rate which, by law, two thirds or more of applicants for their product will be offered. Again, the rate includes all interest, fees and additional charges. Loans come in two basic forms:

unsecured loans and secured loans. An unsecured loan is usually a loan of a smaller amount, typically up to £7,500, where a lender is not bothered about security, as long as the individual can keep up the monthly installment to pay off the loan.

With larger amounts it is very often a lender's practice to secure the loan on property owned by the borrower, and this can be in the form of a second charge on the property. For example, if you own a house that has a mortgage on it, there may be some equity within the property. If the property is worth £100,000 and you have borrowed £50,000, the equity would be £50,000; more than enough for a lender granting a loan of £15,000–£20,000. This is often used for items of a high capital value. The secured lender market typically lends at higher rates than a mortgage lender, but not as much as an unsecured loan costs.

As soon as you see the term 'secured loan' being offered this should flag up that what you are about to enter into may have serious consequences on your wealth and your health. I have seen countless numbers of people get into real financial difficulties by securing their property on a second loan. Unable to keep up the payments, their property was repossessed just because they had gone into arrears on the secondary loan for two or three months, making them homeless. This is an extremely dangerous type of lending. Steer well clear.

Unscrupulous lenders often offer personal loans at exorbitant rates of interest, typically 100% or more per annum, and you should be very, very wary of getting involved in this type of borrowing. A new phenomenon that has arisen recently is where a third-party guarantor will guarantee the payments to the lender if, or when, you fail to make the monthly payments to clear off the loan.

This type of lending typically comes in at rates of a staggering 35% per annum plus, and you need to rely on a relative to guarantee the payments on the loan by signing a legally binding agreement. Again, you should steer clear of this type of lending at all costs as it is ludicrously expensive and fraught with difficulties. Anyone who guarantees a loan for someone they are not familiar with, or who they know to be undisciplined with money, should never consider becoming a guarantor.

Payday-Loans are a great temptation to young people as they start running out of money near the end of the month. With companies advertising 'Payday Loans - Look no further!', you may think your problems are over:

Representative APR: 728.9% (variable). Representative Example: Loan amount £400 for 30 days. Total amount repayable

£459.36. Interest 180.5% p.a. variable. Representative 728.9% APR.

In reality you are going to be a staggering £59.36 worse off each and every time you borrow £400 and you start to play catch –up, borrowing over and over again. There are much better ways of borrowing money if that's what you need to do, and there are also easy ways to manage your money so that, hopefully, you won't have to borrow.

Chapter 5 of this book covers a really simple exercise that will help you make a plan for your money, and I've also set up a website full of additional resources for you if you want to educate yourself even further and take the bull by the horns *[details at the end of the book]*.

Overdrafts

At 18 you can arrange an overdraft facility. You should always agree on this in advance with your bank, as fees for unauthorised borrowing are much higher than for authorised overdrafts. Overdrafts are designed to help in the short term and are not meant to be a long-term loan. They can seriously damage your monthly budget if allowed to get out of control.

An overdraft should be for short-term borrowing or emergencies only. The reason is that it's all too easy to treat it as your spending limit rather than as a last resort. Make sure you don't exceed your overdraft limit and end up paying high fees. Unauthorised overdrafts come with lots of different fees.

The monthly fee can be anything from £5 to £35 or more. A daily fee can be £1 to £6 a day or more, usually up to a fixed limit per month. Transaction fees can be £10 to £25 for every cash withdrawal, direct debit or standing order, cheque or card payment you make, whether or not your bank allows the payment. Overdraft fees can quickly spiral, leaving you without enough money and forcing you to use your overdraft again. If you don't use the right account, they can also be one of the most expensive ways to borrow in the long term.

Students are expected to supplement their maintenance loan through a number of sources, including other forms of credit such as a student bank account overdraft. Every year, as a new tranche of school-leavers descends on university campuses, banks begin their annual fight to claim their cash. But students beware. The generous interest-free overdraft and switching deals on display can turn into a money trap if you fail to keep to the conditions of the account or pay back money back in time.

Students are highly profitable to bank profits as those who open an account during their studies tend to stick for years. This means the banks can in time cross-sell more valuable products like a personal loan or a mortgage, after a student graduates. An interest-free overdraft of up to £1500 might sound like a good deal, but it has to be repaid one day.

Credit Cards

Quite simply, a credit card is a tool for delaying payment for the stuff you buy. You are buying money, and there's a cost. The credit card company lends you the money, and you pay them back at a later date, typically with additional interest. As with most loans, the amount of interest you pay increases depending on how long you take to repay. The first thing to get your head round is the APR.

Credit cards are not necessarily a bad thing if used properly. They can improve your credit score if you manage them well. You'll need a decent credit history to get financial products, such as a mortgage, later on. The better your score, the better the deals you'll be offered.

Pay for items costing over £100 with a credit card and Section

75 protection means the credit card company will refund you if something goes wrong. You can even just pay just the deposit by credit card to be eligible to claim for things like repairs, a retailer going bust, non-delivery, cancellation and fraud.

Learning how to run a credit card account properly can teach you vital money management skills that could see you better off in the future but, like driving a car, a credit card needs handling with care or you could crash and burn. As with student bank accounts, credit cards often come dripping with cashback and rewards. As long as you've got a sound repayment plan, you could be quids in.

The problem that many people, young people and adults alike, find with credit cards is that they are far too easy to use. In the wrong hands, they can be dangerous. They facilitate impulse buying that is unnecessary and unaffordable. We all love a bit of retail therapy from time to time; the good news is that we can still do it without the credit cards. The key is to incorporate it into your plan using the bucket method - when money is accounted for, it is yours to spend how you choose!

Frequently, the reason an individual gets into debt is they borrow the money without fully thinking about how the debt is going to be paid off. They then only pay the minimum balance on the credit card each month. Credit card companies usually want a balance of 5% per month but with credit-card interest rates ranging typically between 15% and 30%, it is very easy to get into a situation where the outstanding balance could take 20 years to clear if only the minimum monthly payments are paid.

Say you bought a handbag with your credit card, you could still be paying for that same handbag twenty years later when it has long since become a vintage item or is sitting in a dustbin. Every month, the balance shows up on your statement when you have long since forgotten what you bought.

People come up with ingenious ways of reducing credit-card temptation including putting the credit card in a plastic container full of water and placing it in the deep freeze in the hope that, by the time it has defrosted, the urge to spend will have dissolved!

Many people use credit cards to purchase 'big ticket' items, spreading the cost over a period of months as they know that they can fund the monthly payments from surplus income rather than waiting until they have saved enough. For example, it would be possible to buy furniture costing £3,000 over a 10-month period by paying back approximately £350 per month, depending on the rate of interest the credit card company charges, and so have the debt cleared off within the ten-month period.

The part that everybody forgets are the high rates of interest that the credit card company charge. At 18%, for every £1,000 borrowed, over the year you have to pay back £1,180. One way around this is to wait until you need to fund the purchase and then apply for a credit card that has an introductory, interest-free period, which can range from six to 18 months. If you plan well in advance, this is an extremely advantageous way of using the credit-card companies 'interest- free offer' to fund a purchase leaving your savings to earn interest.

Store Cards

There are some key differences between a store card and a loyalty card. Many shops offer a loyalty card, like Nectar and

Tesco's, and you are awarded points every time you shop. The points can be used for anything from money off to upgrades on long haul flights.

A store card is essentially a credit card you can only use with just one high street chain or group. As with a credit card, you can use a store card to buy things on credit and pay off the bill at the end of the month. And, as with a credit card, there are charges and interest if you don't pay the minimum payment on time. These can be higher, compared to some regular credit cards.

You may be encouraged to take out a store card at the till when you pay for your shopping. They can come with an initial discount and extras such as money-off vouchers. You must be at least 18 to get one. As with any credit card, you will need to undergo a credit check.

The most important thing to know about store cards is they can be expensive, so handle with care. They can be useful if you're disciplined enough always to pay back what you owe each month. Often other credit options are far better and a lot less expensive. Just because a card says it is gold or platinum, it is still plastic.

 **KEY TAKEAWAYS**

- Credit takes many forms, student loans, bank loans, overdrafts, credit and store cards.

- APR or Annual Percentage Rate is an important acronym to take note of in loan and other contracts as it tells you the total amount the loan will cost you in interest and fees. The higher the APR the more it will cost.

-

  Credit Cards in particular can be pretty dangerous, due to high interest rates. It's possible to use them successfully, but you have to ask yourself first—where is the money to repay coming from?

- Some borrowing, such as student loans can be unavoidable, especially if you don't come from a wealthy family. These loans will also incur interest and you will find you will be paying them for some years to come. If you can save money through part-time or summer work, this can reduce the burden.

- If you don't master money, it's going to master you.

- You cannot spend more than you earn without causing yourself pain.

- Be an individual at all costs

5 Your Future Plan

I am not a fan of the word 'budget' as it means that you have a set amount of money which you can't go over. No two months are the same and no two years are the same when it comes to the demands of money and how you spend it. I prefer the bucket list approach to help visualise spending, saving, and investing as it is more fluid and realistic. Whether you prefer to think in terms of budget or bucket list, it comes down to the same thing; financial planning and a good life.

As young children, with a fixed amount of pocket money, we soon learn how much we can spend each week on say a comic and sweets, and what we need to save for a holiday, a school trip or a treat. As teenagers, we learn from experience how much our weekends and phone accounts are going to cost us and, as a result, we know how much pocket money we need, whether we are given the money or have to earn it. When we move away from home to live on our own, or with friends, or go to college or university, we have a fixed income to juggle for what could be variable expenditures.

We have to learn to manage money even when there is not much of it. It takes commitment and time but with the bucket list to help you plan, anyone can learn and stay in control. By effectively putting your money into 'buckets', each with a different purpose, you can in no time at all answer two key questions: "Do I spend more than I earn?" and "What can I afford to spend?" An instinctive assessment is easy.

If you are eating up your savings or building up debts, bucket 1, the spending bucket, and bucket 2, the savings bucket, are soon empty and you are overspending. If on the other hand, at the end of each month there is still a little in bucket 1 to move to bucket 2, you are in control.

The sensible way to plan is to have a really good idea of what things are going to cost and when you are going to need the money to pay for them. Some expenses are weekly, some monthly and others, such as insurance policies, can be annual. You can start to prioritise what you do with your money to enable you to stick within your means.

It is tempting to try and fool yourself by underestimating your expenditure, or overestimating your income by including the possibility of a gift of money on your birthday, which may or may not transpire. Try to be accurate and always over-estimate what things are likely to cost, erring on the side of caution, so you have money left over rather than be caught short.

As you first become independent, you will probably have a limited income and be restricted in what you can do. As time moves on you will earn more, but your responsibilities may increase. Get into the habit of making weekly, monthly and annual plans, with a built in contingency fund to allow for the unexpected, be that something wonderful like a spontaneous weekend away, or something potentially life changing, like moving home. You will learn to master your money and, in time, reap all the rewards.

Many young people who leave school to go straight to work, or into an apprenticeship, continue to live at home either for free, or giving mum or dad something for their keep, until they can save for a place of their own. You will need a plan, putting money into bucket 2, your savings, until you have enough for a deposit and a few months rent, and can afford to pay your electricity, gas, water and council tax, when you are independent.

Others are not so fortunate and either choose, or need, to leave home as early as possible. If you have been brought up by a foster family or in care, you will receive assistance to help you prepare for independence when you are 16 or 17, and financial help to help you meet your housing costs. You still need to manage your money and plan your personalised bucket list.

If you leave home to go to college or university, you are going to need to rent a room; somewhere to work and sleep. Deposit and rent are usually payable in advance, and so a fair chunk of money has to be paid out for a three-month advance period or, certainly, one month. A laptop and the books you will need have to be bought at the beginning of the year. You will need essentials for your room such as a duvet, bedding, towels, a kettle, pots and pans and other kitchen paraphernalia so that you can cook.

Within a week or two of looking after yourself, you will get to know how much you are going to spend on food. Eating out, takeaways, and a round of drinks need to be allowed for, even when you realise just how much of your weekly food bill is going towards entertainment. Allow a fund for university gigs and balls, birthdays and parties, or you may find yourself missing out on the best social events of the year.

You also need money for sports and hobbies, whether it's playing in a band, gym membership or away matches with your football or cricket team. And a travel allowance for getting around and going back home for the long holidays. Don't forget your mobile phone, whether you pay on a monthly account or pay-as-you-go.

If you are leaving school for work and already have a job lined up, you may know your annual rate of pay. Create your annual bucket list by adding up your expected income but don't forget to deduct your tax and national insurance contributions when figuring out your net pay; your take home pay. See how this compares with your anticipated expenditure using the bucket list exercise included below.

Budgeting accurately is never an easy process, and I have constructed this simple but realistic annual income and expenditure summary, the bucket list exercise, to make monitoring and controlling your finances easier. Bucket 1 and bucket 2, spending and saving, can be visualised as lots of smaller buckets, each with its own purpose, such as 'holiday bucket' and 'birthday present bucket,' if it helps you to simplify the exercise, and keep control. Buckets 3 and 4 are for investments and giving to charity. The beauty of this method is you create what works best for you.

If you are going to college or university, estimate your annual budget by listing all your expected income, whether mum or dad are supporting you, or you need a student loan. Include any savings you will bring with you to university and any grants or scholarships. See how this total compares with your anticipated expenditure by using the bucket list exercises included below. The balance sheet should balance and leave you with spare cash in the bank for saving and doing what you've always wanted to do.

Don't be too optimistic in your first bucket list exercise, and do be aware of how much you actually spend. Writing your expenses down will help you keep a grip on your day-to-day spending, where it's easy to overspend. Your patterns of expenditure will differ significantly between term-time and vacations, and you'll need to budget for this. Above all, remember to keep a check on your finances, so that money worries do not detract from your studying and from getting the most out life at university!

Let's first look at an example of the bucket list exercise filled out, and then you can use the following blank template to complete your own.

BUCKET 1
SPENDING BUCKET

£ PER MONTH

RENT	£ 250
FOOD	£ 80
TRAVEL	£ 25
PERSONAL ITEMS	£ 40
MEMBERSHIPS	£ 10
CLOTHING	£ 15
SOCIALISING	£ 60
TOTAL EACH MONTH	£ 480
INCOME	£ 550
SURPLUS	£ 70

TRANSFERRED TO BUCKET 2

Note: Clothing and socialising can 'kill' a budget. There should always be a surplus of at least 10% of income!!

BUCKET 2
SAVINGS

£ PER MONTH

HOLIDAYS	£ 200
BIRTHDAY PRESENTS	£ 100
CHRISTMAS PRESENTS	£ 150
CAR PURCHASE	£ 250

TOTAL EACH MONTH	£ 700

The faster you grow this bucket the better car you can buy or have more to spend on holiday!!

BUCKET 3
INVESTMENTS

£ PER MONTH

SAVING FOR A 'RAINY DAY' ACCOUNT (INDIVIDUAL SAVINGS ACCOUNT)	£ 50
GIVING UP WORK ACCOUNT (PENSIONS)	£ 50
HOME PURCHASE AMOUNT (USE 'SAVE TO BUY ISA')	£ 100

A minimum of 5% of your income should be placed into this bucket.

This is where the 'magic' of compound interest takes place!!

The government will currently boost your savings by 25% up to a maximum of £3000. So save £12,000 and you get £3000 for nothing!!

The faster you grow this bucket the better car you can buy or have more to spend on holiday!!

BUCKET 4
CHARITY BUCKET

Put what you can into this bucket.

You will put more into this bucket the older you get!!

Aim to put 10% of your income into the charity bucket and top up any donations with gift aid where the government will add 20% to the amount given.

How much I will put in per year   £ _____

SPENDING BUCKET

£ PER MONTH

RENT   £ _____

FOOD   £ _____

TRAVEL   £ _____

PERSONAL ITEMS   £ _____

MEMBERSHIPS   £ _____

CLOTHING   £ _____

SOCIALISING   £ _____

TOTAL EACH MONTH   £ _____

INCOME   £ _____

SURPLUS   £ _____
TRANSFERRED TO BUCKET 2

Note: Clothing and socialising can 'kill' a budget. There should always be a surplus of at least 10% of income!!

BUCKET 2
SAVINGS

£ PER MONTH

HOLIDAYS	£ _____
BIRTHDAY PRESENTS	£ _____
CHRISTMAS PRESENTS	£ _____
CAR PURCHASE	£ _____

TOTAL EACH MONTH   £ _____

The faster you grow this bucket the better car you can buy or have more to spend on holiday!!

BUCKET 3
INVESTMENTS

£ PER MONTH

SAVING FOR A 'RAINY DAY' ACCOUNT   £ _____
(INDIVIDUAL SAVINGS ACCOUNT)

GIVING UP WORK ACCOUNT   £ _____
(PENSIONS)

HOME PURCHASE AMOUNT   £ _____
(USE 'SAVE TO BUY ISA')

A minimum of 5% of your income should be placed into this bucket.

This is where the 'magic' of compound interest takes place!!

The government will currently boost your savings by 25% up to a maximum of £3000. So save £12,000 and you get £3000 for nothing!!

The faster you grow this bucket the better car you can buy or have more to spend on holiday!!

BUCKET 4
CHARITY BUCKET

Put what you can into this bucket.

You will put more into this bucket the older you get!!

Aim to put 10% of your income into the charity bucket and top up any donations with gift aid where the government will add 20% to the amount given.

How much I will put in per year   £ _____

You can get the most out of your money by using your imagination. Young people are full of ingenious ways to make their money go round. One savvy teenager collected hundreds of coupons to buy £600 worth of food for his mum. The bill at the checkout came to £572.16 but once the coupons were factored in, the bill was reduced to just 4p. He regularly scours the internet and papers for vouchers. You can also:

- Take advantage of any discounts, especially student discounts.
- Get to know how to use the library at the earliest opportunity.
- Buy the essential books, or equipment, you need for your course second-hand, and sell them online when you graduate.
- Use the internet to shop around for the best prices.
- Keep an eye open for the best mobile package.
- Shop in local markets, charity shops and the students' union.
- Be careful with heating and lighting.
- Do not hand your debit card to the barman. Pay with cash and keep control if you are on a drunken night out with friends or your hangover could last more than a day when you see the damage to your bank balance.
- Try and buy in bulk if living in a student house, and share costs with your housemates.

- See you are getting the best broadband deal.
- Buy a student cookbook full of inexpensive meals. Learn to cook rather than paying over the odds for ready-made, shop-bought meals. You will become healthier and wealthier.
- Make a sandwich and flask of coffee at home and take it to your place of work or to eat between lectures.
- Share to save whenever you can, particularly on transport.
- Walk or cycle during the day rather than take public transport.
- Question every purchase. Do I really need this?
- Check to see if your belongings can be covered by your family insurance before you fork out for your own policy; essential for expensive items like mobile phones and laptops.

If you get into trouble, don't keep on spending in the vague hope that everything will be fine or hide your head in the sand like an ostrich. Restart your bucket list and don't put off asking for advice. Financial advisers and debt advisers will always have heard a worse story than yours, even if you have been careless. The sooner you deal with any financial difficulties, the better.

Practical Lifestyle Design

Some of you may want a straightforward life. Whatever your job or career, you see yourself one day in a comfortable home, money safely invested, taking regular holidays, and with time to participate in other interests such as climbing Mount Everest, or something less taxing like playing tennis, football or surfing every weekend.

Other young people, concerned about the planet, will want a lifestyle that considers the way we use our resources, our food, energy, shelter and other material and nonmaterial needs. You may want an ecologically sound way of living, cooperating with nature and caring for the earth and its people. You want to reap the benefits for the environment and yourselves, for now, and for generations to come.

And some of you are very ambitious and want to rise to the top of your chosen profession, reaping all the material rewards; saving, investing and spending on life's luxuries.

As time goes by, and you take a step up the ladder to the next rung of your job and your prospects and pay increases or, as you graduate and find employment, everything changes. Once you are in work and have found a place to live, you could be buying a car and putting money into your savings account, bucket 2, for a holiday, a deposit on a house or flat, getting married or living independently.

Even if you don't think buying a property is something you will be able to afford, and choose to go on renting, in time you could have some savings you want to work for you by investing in bucket 3, where they will earn more than in the bank. The earlier you start to make regular savings the better off you will be. It is very difficult when you are young to save, but this is the time when you need to develop the skills and disciplines that will become part of your core culture as you get older. If you don't, you could work all your life chasing wealth and never get anywhere.

Whichever lifestyle you choose from the hundreds of alternatives, one thing is certain; TAX!

The UK's tax system is fiendishly complicated. Many of the rich do everything in their power to evade tax, but there are also legal ways to avoid paying tax. Stories of the trillions held in offshore tax-havens make right-thinking people so outraged they want to pull on tights and go Robin Hood on rich people's assets, and give all the money to the poor. Generally, we just moan about it, but why do we pay tax?

"Taxes are the price we pay for civilisation," said the great US supreme court justice, Oliver Wendell Holmes. The government collects taxes to pay for things that most people use, such as hospitals, doctors, nurses, roads, schools, teachers, libraries, galleries, museums, police and fire protection and our army, navy and air force. There is sales tax on the things you buy and income tax on the money you make and, without tax, there would be anarchy and our civilised way of life would fall apart.

Our taxes are collected on behalf of the government by that formidable department, the HMRC or Her Majesty's Revenue & Customs. There is no escaping from some form of them!

Tax is most commonly collected at source, under the pay as you earn, PAYE, scheme, although some people have to pay by filling out a self-assessment tax return.

If you work for an employer, income tax is usually collected under the PAYE scheme. This means the tax you owe is automatically deducted from your pay by your employer and sent to HMRC. National Insurance is also collected this way.

You will need to fill in a tax return if you are self-employed, a business partner or director, you receive rental income above £2500 a year, you have foreign taxable income, and if you receive other untaxed income and the tax due on it cannot be collected through PAYE.

If you receive some income without tax deducted but you are liable for tax, you have to declare the income to HM Revenue & Customs. Your tax office will tell you how to do this. You pay the extra tax either through a tax return or via an adjustment to your tax code if you are a PAYE taxpayer.

You won't have a P45 if you're starting your first job or you're taking on a second job. Your employer will need to work out how much tax you should be paying on your salary. They may use a 'Starter Checklist' to collect the information, or may collect it another way. The Starter Checklist has questions about any other jobs, benefits or student loans you have. It helps your employer work out your correct tax code before your first payday.

You'll get a P45 from your employer when you stop working for them. Your P45 shows how much tax you've paid on your salary so far in the tax year.

Your P60 shows the tax you've paid on your salary in the tax year, 6 April to 5 April. If you're working for your employer on 5 April, they must give you a P60. They must provide this by 31 May, on paper or electronically. You'll need your P60 to prove how much tax you've paid on your salary to claim back overpaid tax, to apply for tax credits, and as proof of your income if you apply for a loan or a mortgage.

Your employer might give you a copy of your P11D if they used it to tell HM Revenue & Customs about your 'benefits in kind.' Company cars or interest-free loans are called benefits in kind. Your employer does not have to do this, but they must tell you how much each benefit is worth. You might not get a P11D if your employer takes the tax you owe on your benefits out of your pay.

Tax: An overview

If you go straight from school and into work, you will not be paying tax until you earn more than the tax-free allowance of £11,000 per year but you have to make national insurance contributions once you earn more than £155 per week, or £8060 per year. National insurance is the system of compulsory payments by employees and employers to provide state assistance for people who are sick, unemployed, or retired.

Once you start earning, say £11,500 per year, you will be in the first tax bracket, paying basic rate tax of 20%. Your tax will be £300 and your national insurance contributions £425.28 leaving you with £10,774.72 or £897.89 for the month. As your salary increases so does your tax and national insurance contributions.

According to statistics, the average first salary a graduate can expect to earn is £25,000. Everyone has a tax free allowance of £11,000, so the total of taxable earnings is £14,000. The first tax bracket, or basic rate, is 20%. The income tax payable is £ 2,800 per annum. In addition to your tax, you will also pay national insurance.

Class 1 contributions are paid by people who work as employed earners and, with a salary of £25,000, you will be paying £2033 per annum. When calculating your net salary, or take home pay, don't forget to deduct your student loan repayments of £690 per annum on a salary of £25,000, leaving you with £19,477 or £1623.08 per month.

The basic rate of tax continues as your salary rises until you earn more than £43,001. The £1 over the limit takes you into the next tax bracket, the higher rate, which is 40%. This can be a difficult step to comprehend and to negotiate. With a salary of £43,000 your tax will be £6400 but the tax doubles on everything you earn over this threshold.

One day you are taking home x and the next you are celebrating your promotion with a nasty sting in the tail and you are taking home x. I did say our tax system is fiendishly complicated! To overcome this anomaly, you would need to ensure a stepping stone.

One stepping stone, to ease your way into the higher rate tax band is if you earn £43,000 a year and contribute five per cent of this, £2,150, more to your pension, then your taxable salary is just £40,898. This is safely below the higher rate tax limit. But if your salary is £44,000 and you contribute five per cent of this, £2,200, to your pension, then your taxable salary is £41,800.

As the higher rate will now cut in at £41,450, you'll be paying 40 per cent tax on your top £350 of income. You can avoid paying this by paying a little bit more into your pension, although this will leave you with less spending money each month.

You continue at the higher rate of tax until your salary is over £150,000 per annum when you pay the additional rate of 45% but you don't get a Personal Allowance on taxable income over £122,000.

You can claim tax reliefs on pension contributions, maintenance payments, and charitable donations. If you are married or in a civil partnership, you may be able to claim Marriage Allowance to reduce your partner's tax if your income is less than the standard Personal Allowance. From 6 April 2016, most people can earn some income from their savings without paying tax. This is called a Personal Savings Allowance. It applies to each tax year, from 6 April to 5 April the following year.

If your total taxable income is £17,000 or less you won't pay any tax on your savings income, otherwise your allowance depends on which income tax band you're in. If you are in the basic rate band, you have a personal savings allowance of £1000, and if you are in the higher rate band, it is £500. You will pay tax on any income above this at your usual rate of income tax.

The allowance applies to interest from bank and building society accounts, savings and credit union accounts, unit trusts, investment trusts and open-ended investment companies, peer-to-peer lending, government or company bonds, life annuity payments, and some life insurance contracts. Savings already in tax-free accounts like ISAs and some National Savings and Investments accounts don't count towards the allowance.

Capital Gains Tax is a tax on the profit when you sell an asset that has increased in value. It's the gain you make that's taxed, not the amount of money you receive. For example, you bought a painting for £5,000 and sold it later for £25,000. This means you made a gain of £20,000. Some assets are tax-free. You also don't have to pay Capital Gains Tax if all your gains in a year are under your tax-free allowance.

Self-assessment tax returns

If you decide to become self-employed, you will need to inform

Her Majesty's Revenue & Customs and complete a tax return every year. Completing your self-assessment tax return can be relatively straightforward, provided that you have well-organised tax records. These need to include details of any employment income and other types of personal income, such as savings income. You also need details of any reliefs you will be claiming on your income tax return, such as for pension contributions or gifts to charity.

If you are self-employed, you'll need your business tax records. If you run your business as a company, the company will need to complete a separate corporation tax return. If you are in a partnership, you'll need to include details of your share of the partnership income on your self-assessment tax return, but the partnership also needs to file a partnership tax return.

How complicated your self-assessment tax return becomes depends on your circumstances. If you are self-employed, with simple finances and a turnover below £70,000, completing your self-assessment tax return should be relatively easy. HMRC has introduced two simpler income tax schemes for small businesses, 'Cash Basis' and 'Simplified Expenses' designed to make it easier for you to manage your income tax commitments.

A self-employed income tax return is more straightforward if you choose to match your accounting year to the tax year so that you report profits for the year to 5 April. But a different accounting year end may suit you better, for example by deferring tax payments.

Asking for help

The good news about finance is there is so much help available. You should never feel like you have to struggle or be confused about money, and can always ask for help with understanding the best ways to manage money for you, specifically. We are not all mathematical geniuses and it is just as important to know *when* you need help, and *where* to find help, as it is to be a dab hand with a calculator. You could be a whiz at math but still need help making important investment decisions.

This book is designed to untangle all the jargon, facts and myths surrounding money and primarily to illustrate the value of saving. It is not intended to number crunch, except where I use examples to explain complex ideas. Once the numbers start to grow, it is important not just to know the cost of everything but the value.

For example, buying a house or an ISA is potentially an appreciating asset, but buying a car is a depreciating asset; it loses value from the first time you drive it.

There are many useful salary calculators on the internet to help you work out your take home pay, to see what you will earn when you have found a job. Pop in your details and up come the facts. The Prince's Trust have lots of online support. They have teamed up with the Money Advice Service, MAS, to bring you a range of top tools to help support your finances. As your salary increases, and your lifestyle choices begin to take shape, your finances might become more and more complicated and you could need help making the right decisions; decisions which could help you save and help you earn more.

On the other hand, you may find you have little discipline to save. Just as all your other new year resolutions fail, in spite of your good intentions, bucket no. 1 is running on empty as the tills keep on going cha-ching, cha-ching. Just as some people hire personal trainers to ensure that they have regular exercise to keep fit, or a singer needs a voice coach, so it is with money.

The one way that you can have a stress-free life with money is to set up a formal financial coaching arrangement with a financial coach. Initially, a coach will set up a programme in the form of a lifetime financial plan, taking into account your prefered lifestyle. With regular meetings, your coach will ensure that your plans remain on track and that you will not get into debt along the way. A financial coach will also be brutally honest with you when it comes to expenditure and will always raise the question, "do you really need it?" to avoid excess expenditure and encourage the discipline of saving.

Financial coaching is a relatively new idea only a few people in the UK, Europe, and the USA have adopted. The concept started in Australia and is a growing part of the Australian financial advice profession. It is showing better results than any other form of financial help to date. With a financial coach holding your hand every step of the way, you will not only receive support but they will help you to believe in yourself, relieve anxiety and turn your dreams into reality.

Many people consider you need to be rich, or on a high salary to afford a financial adviser. The opposite is true. A good financial adviser will be ensuring you can pay their fees by stopping you from making bad decisions, saving you money, and by helping you make the right choices, earning more. A win-win situation. As soon as you need to consider your pension, a mortgage, and what to do with your savings, you are old enough to consult with a financial adviser. And, as at 22 years old you will have to make some very grown-up decisions regarding your pension contributions, what better time to get some help.

Pensions

It's understandable if you glaze over when I ask you ask you to think about retirement and pensions. I am not asking you to think about old age, but to understand the world of work you are about to enter. With automatic enrollment due to see millions of workers put into a workplace pension scheme from the age of 22, you need to understand the importance of saving for a pension and the consequences of opting out.

Take the example of two young men who want to save up for their retirement but, having different lifestyles and mindsets, do so in two different ways. The first, John, at the age of 20, is earning £21,500 per annum. After tax and deductions and his student loan repayment, he is taking home £1451. He saves £100 per month. It is difficult at first to find the money but, with careful planning, he can still afford an annual trip to Glastonbury and, as his salary increases over time he doesn't miss a £100.

At 40 years old, with the demands of a family, holidays and buying the dream home, he will stop saving. However, he leaves his saving fund, bucket no 3, which now amounts to more than £40,000, to continue to grow until he is 60. If we assume an interest rate of 5%, he will have a fund of nearly £108,000 which will have cost him just £24,000.

The second man, David, is in exactly the same position but has a different lifestyle and mindset. He spends every penny of his £1451 monthly income and does not save. By the time he is 30, although his income has increased dramatically, he has started a family and his spending soars. He needs a family car and the deposit for his first house.

David delays putting anything into Bucket no. 3 and saving for retirement until he is 40 years old but, playing catch-up, he saves twice as much as John, £200 per month, until he is 60. Assuming the same 5% rate of interest on his fund, David would have nearly £81,500 which will have cost him 48,000.

On face value, it looks as if John saved half as much as David for his old age, but you will see the staggering difference in the two scenarios all because of the power of compound interest and starting young. As Albert Einstein said, 'Compound interest is the eighth wonder of the world. He who understands it earns it, he who doesn't, pays it.'

To help more people save for their retirement, the government has made major changes to how workplace pensions operate. In the past, it was up to workers to decide whether they wanted to join their employer's pension scheme but by 2018 all employers will have to automatically enroll their eligible workers into a workplace pension scheme unless the worker opts out. As a result, many more people will be able to build up savings to help cover their retirement needs.

There is a minimum total amount that has to be contributed by you, by your employer, and by the government, in the form of tax relief. The total minimum contribution is currently set at 2% of your earnings; 0.8% from you, 1% from your employer, and 0.2% as tax relief.

The minimum contribution applies to anything you earn over £5,824 up to a limit of £43,000. This includes overtime and bonus payments. So if you were earning £18,000 a year, your contribution would be a percentage of £12,176; the difference between £5,824 and £18,000.

The reason these changes are being introduced is that too few of us are saving as much as we should for retirement. In general, there's a big gap between the kind of lifestyle we hope to enjoy in retirement and the kind of lifestyle that we're on track to be able to afford.

Don't rely on the State Pension to cover you in retirement. From April 2016 the new State Pension will be £155.65 per week, far below the kind of income most people say they hope to retire on.

Buying a home

After your pension, the first very grown up thing you may decide you want is to buy a house. Over the past few years, the perils of the mortgage market have been graphically illustrated, and the prospects of obtaining a home loan were very limited.

Mortgages that only require a deposit of 15%, 10% and even 5% of a property's value are starting to appear once more at affordable rates. And, as rents rise, more young people want to buy a property. However, house prices, even for first-time buyers, are very high as there are not enough properties to go round.

If you do find a house you can afford, the question is, how do you safely navigate through the mortgage maze, finding out what types of mortgage are out there and what is best for you? Preparing for a mortgage starts early, so make sure you keep your finances in order from the moment you open your first bank account. If you have never had any credit in the past, it can be worth taking out a credit card and using it sparingly, making sure it is paid off in full at the end of each month. This helps to build your credit score.

Lenders like to see your address history for the past three years, pay slips from the past three months, and your last P60 or three years of accounts, your last three months of bank statements, and full details of any loans or credit cards you may have.The basis of any mortgage, whether you opt for a fixed, variable or tracker rate, is how you intend to repay the loan. In essence, there are two repayment options:

Capital and interest, or repayment, mortgages work as standard loans do. The monthly payments include not only the interest due on the loan but also little bits of the capital balance. As the loan begins to reduce, slowly at first, so the interest element becomes smaller while the capital repayments become a larger part. At the end of the term, providing the repayments have been made every month, you know the loan will be paid off without risk.

Interest-only. This loan does not include any capital repayment at all, so the capital does not reduce unless you overpay each month, or you set up some other savings, such as an ISA, to grow over the years to repay the loan. There is a risk involved in this method as if you do not have sufficient funds available to repay the loan at the end of the term, you may have to sell your property.

Once the repayment method is decided, there are lots of individual rate choices. It is important to work out which product would be best for your circumstances and often the cheapest looking products may have the highest fees or not be very flexible. All this could cost money in the longer term.

Fixed rates are as simple as they sound. This is where you agree to fix at the same rate for a set period, normally two, three or five years. As there will be no changes to your mortgage payments, you can budget better.

Tracker and variable mean the rate can change at any time owing to decisions by the Bank of England or by your lender. The most popular type of variable rate is the tracker mortgage. These track the Bank of England base rate over a period, from two years to the whole length of the mortgage. For example, if the product is set at 2% above the Bank rate, which is at 0.5% now, the initial rate would be 2.5%. However, if the Bank rate increased to 1.5%, payments would then be based on 1.5% plus 2% which equals 3.5%, hence the greater risk element. Of course, this can also move downwards, reducing your current rate.

Assurance or Insurance?

There are various scenarios you need to consider as you grow older and your job prospects and income increase. You may be fluid in your approach to work, or you may have a very fixed idea of what you want out of life, but you can't always predict what will happen along the way. Life is like a game of snakes and ladders. One minute you are climbing and, at the throw of a dice, you are back where you started. There are only two certainties in life; death and taxes!

One young woman, Liz, graduated from University and spent the next five years working on a Greek island, learning the language and enjoying the sun. Aware her career was going nowhere, she returned to London to work for a property company. She quickly paid off her student loan and sensibly put money into her savings and her pension. As her salary increased, she was able to move to a lovely flat, buy some beautiful furniture, invest in a few paintings and travel overseas four times a year. Liz was careful with her money and looked the picture of success.

Ten years later, Liz took a more interesting job and a pay rise and left to spend Christmas in Portugal. Overnight her life changed. She fell off a stairway and broke her heel; a very nasty fracture which left her in great pain, unable to walk. Her new employers declined to give her sick pay. Liz had only been with the company two months and their policy only paid out after two years of employment. Suddenly her only income was her statutory sick pay, a government benefit, which didn't even cover her bills, let alone pay her rent and put food on the table.

With all her other outgoings, and believing herself covered by a company policy, Liz had not taken out a personal insurance policy. She immediately had to resign her job, advise her landlord she was giving up her tenancy agreement and move out of London to the countryside, where she could live less expensively.

Fortunately, Liz had enough savings to enable the move and, using her skills and contacts, found a job working online at home, which she fitted in between her physiotherapy and hospital visits. Her new salary is a third of what she was earning before her accident. Liz has been able to modify her lifestyle, adjust her bucket List and is on her feet. However, she has used up all the money she was saving to buy a house and is back on the first rung in the game of snakes and ladders. The moral of the story is make sure you are covered. Don't leave anything to chance.

The first option is to set up an emergency fund to cater for perhaps one or two years' loss of net spendable income, and this is where your own personal budgeting comes into force as now you have an idea of how much of your core expenditure you need for basic needs. If your basic needs are around £1,000 per month, then you need £12,000 a year, or £24,000, being two years' expenditure; a better safety net. If your needs are only £500 per month, then you will need £12,000 for that two-year period.

The second option is to insure against the possibility of illness and disability by taking out what is known as an income protection policy. These policies are governed by four things: the age you are when you take them out, what your occupation is, whether it is a low-risk occupation or a high-risk occupation, the age you want the cover to run to, and the waiting period before the benefits are payable. Most people have this type of policy running through to their retirement age, which is currently 66 but is rising all the time. Soldiers, fire-fighters, and off-shore oil workers can expect to pay more than teachers, office and shop workers.

The other factor is how long you have to wait until the policy benefits are paid out. This is typically 13 weeks, six months, or a year. If your employer pays your full salary for the first six months, then a six-month waiting period would be appropriate. If you are self-employed, a waiting period of thirteen weeks would be more appropriate, but you will need savings to cover the interim period.

The best type of policy is one that is index-linked with the benefit on an annual basis, as well as payments. What you don't want is to take out a policy on a level basis, get to age forty and find that your income has doubled. The policy will pay out but does not cater for inflation. You quickly find your policy only covers half of your core expenditure.

A variation on this type of cover is called Critical Illness Insurance. This insurance pays out a lump sum based on the diagnosis of a variety of critical illnesses. It was designed to provide an emergency fund and is geared to paying off debt, such as a mortgage, and aid recovery as the result of less stress. I would encourage every young person to have at least £50,000 of critical illness cover that has the capability to run through to age seventy. The cost of this when you are younger is peanuts compared to the benefits it gives.

Redundancy is traumatic as, psychologically, it can feel like rejection, undermining your confidence. Redundancy may bring with it a financial compensation package, depending on the number of years you have worked for an employer. If you are employed for a short time, no money will be available, but if you have been employed for a few years, the rule of thumb is that you will get a week's income for every year you have been employed.

While everybody needs a rainy-day savings fund, you should

be aware that you may need a very significant sum to match the sort of payouts that can be offered by policies like life insurance, critical illness cover, income protection and life assurance. So, Life Assurance or Life Insurance?

The average man in the street assumes that Life Insurance and Life Assurance are names for the same thing. How wrong they are! Life Insurance and Life Assurance perform different financial roles and are poles apart in cost. Life Insurance provides you with insurance cover for a specific period of time, known as the policy's "term".

Then, if you were to die whilst the policy is in force, the insurance company pays out a tax-free sum. If you survive to the end of the term, the policy is finished and has no residual value whatsoever. It only has a value if there is a claim, in that context it's just like your car insurance.

Life Assurance is different. It is a hybrid mix of investment and insurance. A Life Assurance policy pays out a sum equal to the higher of either a guaranteed minimum underwritten by the policy's insurance provisions or its investment valuation. Each year the insurance company adds an annual bonus to the guaranteed value of your life assurance policy and there is normally an extra bonus at the end. Therefore, as the years go by your life assurance policy increases in value as the investment bonuses accumulate.

If you were to die during a Life Assurance policy's term, the policy pays out the higher of either the guaranteed minimum sum or the accumulated value of the annual investment bonuses. However, if you are still living when the policy terminates, you usually get a bigger payout. This is because with most insurance companies, an additional terminal bonus is awarded. There is a also a specialised form of life assurance called "Whole of Life". These policies remain in force for as long as you live.

When you are young, free and single, the thought of life assurance will never cross your mind. Life assurance is typically bought to protect a family by paying off a mortgage or loans and providing extra income. If you get married or are in a partnership, you will enter into financial commitments together, perhaps go on to have children, and it is wise to ensure the lifestyle of each partner against their premature death.

I have witnessed too many occasions where a mother has to go back to work and put her children into nursery care after her husband has died at a tragically young age, all because of a lack of a life assurance policy.

Life Assurance rates get more expensive the older you are. This is just a fact of life, based on the risk that the life assurance company will take when looking at your proposal. A typical example of straightforward life assurance through to age 70, for an amount of £100,000, would be at age twenty x amount per month; at age thirty x amount per month; at age forty x amount per month; and age fifty x amount per month.

You will see there is a rapid increase the older you get. The other big benefit of buying life assurance at an early age is that you are generally fitter. Typical conditions, such as high blood pressure and diabetes, may occur as we get older, and are a reason for life assurance companies to increase the premiums, or to decline to insure you altogether.

Before committing to buying a property, investing in a pension, accident and life insurance policies, you need to know you are getting the best possible deal, and you are not wasting money unnecessarily. Being optimistic or oblivious to the consequences of not having a safety net can cost you dearly.

If you can save money in any way, whether it is saving money on buying something because you can get it cheaper or have someone contribute to your pension fund, you should always look to do this. If you have a mortgage, instead of paying 12 monthly payments of £400 per month, you can pay £400 every four weeks. You will never notice the difference in paying that amount of money as, psychologically, it appears to be at the same frequency, but the beauty is that instead of paying 12 months per year, you are paying 13. Over a 25-year mortgage, this could save you two and a half years of principal payments, thousands of pounds, and you will own your house outright much quicker.

If you work for a company that will match your pension payments up to certain levels, you should always try and pay the maximum. If, for example, the company will put in the same amount as you do, up to say 5%, it makes sense to find that 5% each month and have the company match it to make use of what is essentially free money.

The E.U.

You were born into the European Union, the EU. The EU is an economic and political partnership involving 28 European countries. It began after World War II to foster economic co-operation, with the idea that countries which trade together are more likely to avoid going to war with each other.

It has since grown to become a "single market" allowing goods and people to move around as if the member states were one country. It has its own parliament and sets rules in a wide range of areas including the environment, transport, consumer rights and even things such as mobile phone charges.

Britain was made a member state in 1973. Following the referendum in June 2016, the majority voted to leave and go it alone. Although, as Lord Ashcroft's poll indicates, more young people voted to remain in Europe than to leave, the vote decided Britain will withdraw from the EU and your generation will have to deal with the consequences.

How different age groups voted

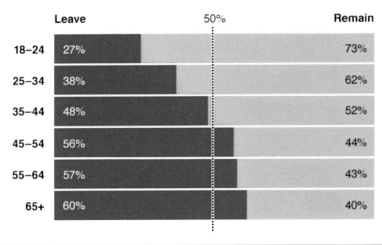

	Leave	50%	Remain
18–24	27%		73%
25–34	38%		62%
35–44	48%		52%
45–54	56%		44%
55–64	57%		43%
65+	60%		40%

Source: Lord Ashcroft Polls

BBC

A comment on the Financial Times website was widely shared. Young people's freedom of movement has been snatched away from, "a generation that was already drowning in the debts of our predecessors".

The effects of leaving the EU on your finances and way of life will only become apparent over time, but you can still use your passport. It is a British document. There is no such thing as an EU passport so it will stay the same, until it's up for renewal.

 **KEY TAKEAWAYS**

- If you fail to plan, you plan to fail. So the saying goes. There are many areas of your future life where planning will be necessary, so it's good to get a head start on it.

- Plan your spending around the bucket list.

- As well as controlling what you spend, you can also have control over costs in different ways. For example, shopping around for the best deals (you don't always have to pay full retail), using coupons to save on food, and cutting down expenses—walk or cycle rather than paying for transport.

- Tax is unavoidable once you begin earning over £11,000 per year. There are legal ways you can reduce tax you pay such as tax reliefs on pension contributions, maintenance payments, and charitable donations—so always take advantage of them.

- Pensions may not seem relevant when you're young, but it's another thing that you will get more out of if you start early.

- Your life is yours to create

- Thinking ahead, setting goals and taking action will get you there

6 Myth Buster

Dream with me for a minute. Imagine what our world would look like when schools get serious about educating money-smart teenagers. The student loan debt would disappear, credit card companies would be out of business, and we would have the resources to feed the hungry, house the homeless, and save the planet. But even if you can't solve all the world's financial problems right now, you can begin to make a difference by debunking the common money myths you might be tempted to believe.

There are more myths about money than about all the ancient Greek gods and goddesses put together, including Croesus. Rich as Croesus, the mythical King of Lydia, was supposedly the richest man on earth.

Thanks to the fact that most teenagers rely on their uninformed peers to answer their pressing financial questions, there is plenty of misinformation passed around which makes it even harder for you to get the facts straight about money and other personal finance topics including credit scores, banking, and taxation. As Mark Twain said, "It ain't what you don't know that gets you into trouble. It's what you know for sure that just ain't so."

The most common myths we need to bust are:

Teenagers don't need to worry about money.
A recent survey found one in four teenagers don't know the difference between a debit card and a credit card. By the time you have read to end of the book, I hope you are a lot better informed and well equipped to start taking control. Read on and we will bust more common money myths you might be tempted to believe.

Teenagers aren't old enough to budget. Here's the deal: If you're old enough to *spend* money, you're old enough to *budget* money.

Credit cards teach teenagers how to handle money. Credit cards can teach young adults to spend money they don't have. You need to learn how to handle a credit card with care.

Teenagers don't pay tax. Not true. Adults and teenagers alike pay tax once your income exceeds the personal allowance, currently £11,000 per annum.

The Bank deducts my tax. No. Your employer will deduct your tax from your earnings, but you will have to declare any income from savings, your unearned income, yourself.

The car I am saving for costs £1500. No, it doesn't. It costs £1500 plus insurance, tax, maintenance and petrol.

The state pension is £800 a week. Teenagers recently quizzed about their pensions knowledge were asked what they considered to be a reasonable state pension. They answered £800 a week. This ambitious suggestion is equivalent to a salary of nearly £42,000 a year. The actual figure is currently £155 a week.

The government will give me a pension. Seven out of 10 of teenagers think the government will provide most of their income when they retire, and eight out of 10 think they will retire in their mid-60s. In reality, the goalposts keep moving, and you will probably be much older. A wake-up call to teenagers to get saving. If you want to retire before you reach the age of 70 or 75, and have more than the minimum to live on, you will need a pension policy or investments to make up the difference.

There's good debt and bad debt. Good debt is a contradiction, an oxymoron. You can't have a good debt any more than you can have a ground pilot. If anyone tries to tell you otherwise, run the other way! Being a teenager is hard enough without worrying about debt. Monthly payments are draining on your bank account and your spirit.

If it looks like a duck, swims like a duck, then it probably is a duck. False. Many people are fooled by all the spoof emails we receive trying to scam us out of our bank details. They often look totally authentic, replicating major well-known companies down to the last detail, but the genuine companies you might have accounts with, now or in the future, will never ask you for your bank details by email.

Never a borrower nor lender be. True. If a friend asks if they can borrow money from you consider first if you can afford to make a gift of the money. Even with the best of intentions, they might never repay you.

Having busted the adult myth, teenagers are irresponsible and shown you are far more capable and smart than given credit for, there is one more myth we need to debunk, perhaps the most important myth of all: Money can't buy happiness.

Does Money Buy Happiness?

The cliché, 'money can't buy happiness,' is rarely questioned. The expression tends to be bandied about by those who have never gone without. "I've tried hard to care about money," a young Chelsea Clinton once bragged, "but I couldn't." No matter how convinced you are by the idea that money can't buy happiness, the research shows almost the complete opposite.

Although money is clearly no guarantee of happiness, as a general rule, the better off we are financially, the happier we are. The link between money and wellbeing is woven into our psyche. Money doesn't just protect us from daily stress and anxiety but actually buys us the most basic of our needs; human connection. The higher your income, the less likely you are to experience loneliness.

Money *does* matter. For most workers, real income has barely risen for decades. The UK is the world's sixth largest economy, yet one in five of the UK population live below our official poverty line, meaning that they experience life as a daily struggle. Money isn't a perk to our wellbeing. It's at the very heart and soul of it.

And instead of being ashamed to admit money matters, we

should be shouting it from the rooftops, using it as a headline in every newspaper; Money makes us happy! Pretending money is of little consequence doesn't make us enlightened, altruistic, or morally superior. It makes us oblivious; it makes us clueless.

Even the most altruistic, selfless people in society need money to make others happy. The sainted nun, Mother Teresa, raised millions to help the poor and sick in India where she established her Missionaries of Charity. "What is of the poor is mine and what is mine, is for the poor," she said, as she prevented local administrators from demolishing homes built for the slum dwellers.

Global inequality is growing, with half the world's wealth now in the hands of just 1% of the population; currently 1% of 7.4 billion people. It is worth considering a person needs only £2,100 to be in the wealthiest 50% of world citizens. About £47,500 secures a place in the top 10%, while the top 1% have more than £526,000 each. The study defines wealth as the value of assets including property and stock market investments

About 3.4 billion people, just over 70% of the global adult population, have a wealth of less than £7000. A further one billion are in the £7000 - £70,000 bracket. Each of the remaining 383 million adults has wealth of more than £70,000.

A staggering 54,000 people in the UK have a wealth of more than £50 million. The UK has the third-highest number of these "ultra-high net worth" individuals in the world.

As the poor get poorer, and the rich get richer, what do the millionaires, and billionaires do with all their money?

Saving the Best for Last

It is probably apparent to some of you, we haven't discussed bucket No 4, the 'giving' bucket. As a nation, we are very generous so you probably don't need much encouragement to put something aside to give away. The Children in Need appeal raised the staggering sum of £37.1 million last year, and the UK people raised £87 million for the Nepal Earthquake Appeal.

A 10-year-old girl from Cornwall raised more than £40,000 for terminally ill children. Madison Glinski took the streets of St Ives with her violin to raise money for a children's hospice. She set an initial target of £500 but has now raised £40,500.

Every day we hear of people's extraordinary efforts to help others by running marathons or cycling around the world, raising money. Giving does buy happiness; happiness for others, and happiness for ourselves. Buying a lottery ticket in the hope you will become one of the few to hit the jackpot gives money to many worthy causes across the UK. Your intentions might not be selfless but your loss, when you don't win, is someone else gain.

Some of you will have been brought up in a culture of giving. Orthodox Jews are asked to give 10% of their income to charity. Giving to those who deserve it is part of Muslim character and one of the Five Pillars of Islamic practice. Many Christians, of different denominations: Church of Scotland, Church of England or Catholic, make donations to their Church.

Some people who have migrated to the UK from much poorer countries regularly send money to their families overseas. And many people have a favourite cause or charity they frequently support by setting up a direct debit to make monthly contributions. Whatever form your 'giving' takes, you can save with bucket no. 4, the giving bucket.

Just as important, many people both qualified and unqualified, give of their time, and give of their skills. These include surgeons who repair cleft palates in young children or carry out cataract operations in the eyes of the elderly. Engineers who travel to Africa to build fresh water-pumping stations to alleviate famine and poverty in those countries, or young people who put up tents after tsunamis, earthquakes, and floods, to give shelter to the homeless, or use their gap year to teach in Africa. People who volunteer for these missions forgo income from their jobs to provide their services to these extremely good causes.

To answer the question, what do the millionaires, and billionaires do with all their money; they give it away! However, as the TV presenter, Anne Robinson, once said, "Money is something we are all fascinated and governed by, and yet it is very British not to actually talk about it." Many of the rich and famous do not advertise their generosity. They often conceal it, or distance themselves, with trustees handling their philanthropy to maintain their anonymity.

Dispelling yet another age-old myth, Scotsmen are tight with their money, Andrew Carnegie, who was as 'rich as Croesus', richer than Bill Gates, the co-founder of Microsoft, gave away the equivalent of $225 billion, yes billion, to charities, foundations and universities!

Carnegie, born in Dunfermline, Scotland, was an industrialist in Victorian times and probably the richest man ever. As he started to accumulate wealth he developed the philosophy that he was merely a temporary custodian of his money, a caretaker and, just as the money he made flowed in, it would flow back out. Carnegie saw it as his responsibility to make sure that his money was used in a sustainable way. In 1889 he wrote an article proclaiming 'the gospel of wealth,' which called on the rich to use their wealth to improve society.

His article stimulated a wave of philanthropy throughout his rich friends. The Carnegie Foundation, rich with the cash that he left them, still provides funds and grants to both individuals and organisations to do good throughout the world. With Apollo's help, the mythical Croesus is said to have lived happily ever after; let us hope the legendary Carnegie did the same.

As Carnegie's philosophy lives on, some of the world's wealthiest individuals have pledged to give away the majority of their wealth both during their lifetimes and after their death. Among those who have set up a modern 'Carnegie' philanthropic cause are Bill and Melinda Gates of Microsoft wealth. The Bill and Melinda Foundation will give away their entire fortune. Warren Buffet, one of the wealthiest investors who has ever lived, has made a similar pledge. These two men have inspired hundreds of other industrialists and entrepreneurs to promise to do the same.

One of our most famous philanthropists, who has not only given us her literary genius with her enthralling, magical Harry Potter stories, and her inspiring philosophy, but has given away a huge part of her wealth, is J.K. Rowling.

Besides giving to Gingerbread, a charity working with lone parents and their children, she supports a number of other charities and causes through her charitable trust, Volant. This includes funding for research into the causes, treatment and possible cures of Multiple Sclerosis, channeled via the Anne Rowling Regenerative Neurology Clinic.

Talking about her new charity, J K Rowling said, "Lumos has a single, simple goal: to end the institutionalisation of children worldwide by 2050. This is ambitious, but achievable. It is also essential. Eight million voiceless children are currently suffering globally under a system that, according to all credible research, is indefensible. We owe them far, far better. We owe them families."

Named after the light-giving spell in the Harry Potter books,

Lumos is an international non-profit organisation that helps countries reform their services for disadvantaged children.

Not only is this remarkable woman generous with her wealth, her time and her caring but, as you imagine what your future will be, now I have told you how to take care of your money, she has given you a message,

"We do not need magic to transform our world; we carry all the power we need inside ourselves already."

I hope you've enjoyed reading all about money and how you can master yours. You don't need to wait until you have left school or completed your education. You can begin to take control now, before you make the decision to fly the nest and become independent. Money has the power to help you achieve your wildest dreams, no matter how big or small they might be. You have your whole life ahead of you and the fun is just beginning.

Your generation, and those who follow, have the potential to change the world for the better. When mastered, your money will set you free and enable you to live life on your own terms. Who knows what wonderful experiences or challenges will come your way in the future, but I wish you all good luck for the journey you're about to embark on.

To continue learning and for more support, you can visit my website which contains resources created specifically for you: www.themoneyinstructionbook.com

I'm also happy to answer any questions, hear your thoughts or concerns,and provide more knowledge and insight to help you. You can contact me through the website.

WHAT NOW?

In reading this book you've completed 3 very important first steps to being financially savvy before you leave home.

1 You now have an understanding of the basics; what money really is, how best to use it and tips and traps to avoid.

2 You've started your own financial plan, by completing the Bucket List exercise.

3 You understand more about your own natural approach to money and the opportunities and risks involved by completing the Money Mindset Scorecard.

 ## SO WHERE DO YOU GO FROM HERE?

How do you maintain this organisation and remain able to independently manage your finances now you're a young adult?

We've put together a host of different resources to help you not just today, but over the months and years ahead. We want you to feel confident about your financial choices and equipped to make the right decisions for you and your future.

Continue your good work by keeping in touch with us and downloading the free resources we've created for you at

www.themoneyinstructionbook.com

About The Author

Max Horne is one of the world's leading financial advisers. He is a member of Million Dollar Round Table's Top of the Table, who represent the top 1% of elite financial advisers worldwide. He runs his financial planning practice from Dunfermline, Scotland, the birthplace of the world renowned philanthropist, Andrew Carnegie.

He entered the financial services profession in 1979, having seen his late father in law die without any life assurance or pensions and watching his mother in law having to sell the family home and move back into rented accommodation just to survive. He has been on a mission ever since to ensure that what he witnessed should never happen to anyone else.

He is thoroughly convinced that financial education is sadly lacking in schools in the United Kingdom. Despite successive governments paying lip service to this nothing has been done to tackle the culture of overspending and debt that is rife in society today.

He hopes this book will create some good habits in the youngsters of today as, up to now, 'money doesn't come with instructions'.